Partnership out of Conflict

To Keith

Best wishes

Alexander [illegible]

Partnership Out of Conflict

The Emergence of the Educational Institute of Scotland's Learning Representatives

Alex Alexandrou

humming earth

Published by

Humming Earth
an imprint of
Zeticula
57 St Vincent Crescent
Glasgow
G3 8NQ
Scotland.

http://www.hummingearth.com
admin@hummingearth.com

ISBN-13 978-1-84622-12-2 Hardback
ISBN-10 1 84622 012 8 Hardback

ISBN-13 978-1-84622-013-5 Paperback
ISBN-10 1 84622 013 0 Paperback

Dedicated to the memory of

Pat Davies (1948-2007)

Contents

Preface

This book has been inspired by both my personal and professional experiences of working with trade unions and within education. I have worked for a number of trade unions and representative bodies as well at Ruskin College. Through this work, I have seen at first hand the benefits of trade union involvement in education and training. In turn my experiences of studying and working within the higher education sector for the past twenty years have moulded me into an educational researcher with a special interest in the continuing professional development of all types of employees. The opportunity to study the Educational Institute of Scotland's (EIS) Learning Representatives (LRs) scheme was too good an opportunity to turn down. It fused my passion for trade unions and promoting education and training at all times. It is my firm belief that this type of representative is here to stay, will change the face of British trade unionism and genuinely rekindle the learning bug in many people.

Trade unions have historically been involved in education and training in the workplace and this activity has gained greater credence and importance due to Union Learning Representatives (ULRs). ULRs are a relatively recent phenomenon and a new category of unpaid lay representation with statutory rights who operate within the workplace. They are part of the present New Labour administration's drive to expand and improve lifelong learning and continuing professional development (CPD) in order to create the new *learning society*. In Scotland, the *McCrone Report* (2000), particularly its CPD recommendations and the subsequent *21st Century Agreement* (Scottish Executive Education Department (SEED, 2001)) has added impetus to the role of ULRs within the teaching profession. This book examines how the EIS which represents the overwhelming majority of teachers in Scotland, has taken up the challenge and launched a LRs initiative with the expressed desire that these representatives work to advise, broker and facilitate improved CPD opportunities for their colleagues, particularly in relation to Chartered Teacher (CT) status.

Through a case study approach, the book examines who the first cohort of EIS LRs are; what their role is; how these representatives are developing within the EIS; the impact they are having in relation to their colleagues' CPD and considers how effective this policy is in practice particularly in relation to their cynical colleagues.

Acknowledgements

This book draws on my doctoral thesis and I would like to take this opportunity to thank all those who helped me with my original research and for turning it into this current publication.

Firstly to all the Educational Institute of Scotland's (EIS) Learning Representatives, National Officials and other stakeholders from the Scottish Education sector who participated in my research: without them this book would not have come to fruition. I would like to mention in particular the significant assistance I have had from Lyn McClintock, the EIS Learning Representatives Administrator, Simon Macaulay, EIS Assistant Secretary and Veronica Rankin EIS National Officer Education and Equalities. Their guidance and facilitation have proved invaluable in ensuring the research has progressed smoothly and that I have been able to access all available sources and persons that this study required.

I want to thank my doctoral supervisory team of John Dwyfor Davies and John Lee who have been supportive, incisive with their observations and patient. I hope I have produced a book that is a testament to their belief in me. Thanks also go my EdD examiners, Gay Attwood and Peter Fairbrother whose comments on my original thesis have helped to shape this book.

Next, I want to thank my wife Clare for her support, encouragement, patience and love; my family, particularly my parents for inspiring and guiding me through life; my colleagues on the EdD at the University of the West of England who have befriended me, opened up my mind to new ideas and concepts, and will be friends for life and to all my friends, too numerous to name here for their advice, guidance and support over the years.

Finally, but not least, Louie, my son, this is for you.

Glossary

ACAS	Advisory, Conciliation and Arbitration Service
AGM	Annual General Meeting
AMICUS	The Manufacturing, Technical and Skilled Persons' Union
APL	Accredited Prior Learning
BERA	British Educational Research Association
CIPD	Chartered Institute of Personnel and Development
CPD	Continuing Professional Development
CT	Chartered Teacher
DES	Department for Education and Science
DFEE	Department for Education and Employment
DFES	Department for Education and Skills
DHT	Deputy Head Teacher
DTI	Department for Trade and Industry
EDD	Professional Doctorate in Education
EDAP	Employee Development Assistance Programme
ELLD	Enterprise and Lifelong Learning Department
EIS	Educational Institute of Scotland
EU	European Union
FE	Further Education
FSS	Framework for Staged Support
GMB	General and Municipal Boilermakers Union
GTCS	General Teaching Council Scotland
HEI	Higher Education Institution
HMIE	Her Majesty's Inspectorate of Education
HRM	Human Resource Management
HT	Head Teacher
ILA	Individual Learning Account
INSET	In-Service Training
IT	Information Technology
LA	Local Association

LEA	Local Education Authority
LR	Learning Representative
LRD	Labour Research Department
LTS	Learning and Teaching Scotland
MSF	Manufacturing Science and Finance Union
NAGCELL	National Advisory Group for Continuing Education and Lifelong Learning
NHS	National Health Service
NUT	National Union of Teachers
PCS	Public and Commercial Services' Union
PD	Professional Development
PDR	Personal Development Record
PGCOW	Post Graduate Certificate in Workplace Organisation
PT	Principal Teacher
SEED	Scottish Executive Education Department
SEJ	Scottish Education Journal
STUC	Scottish Trades Union Congress
SULF	Scottish Union Learning Fund
TEI	Teacher Education Institution
TES	Times Educational Supplement
TUC	Trades Union Congress
TURU	Trade Union Research Unit
UK	United Kingdom
ULF	Union Learning Fund
ULR	Union Learning Representative
UNISON	The Trade Union for People Delivering Public Services
USA	United States of America

1

INTRODUCTION

> 'Education is not a profitable business but a costly one; nay, even the best attainments of it are always unprofitable, in any terms of coin. No nation ever made its bread either by great arts, or its great wisdoms. By its minor arts or manufactures, by its practical knowledges, yes: but its noble scholarship, its noble philosophy, and its noble art, are always to be bought as a treasure, not sold as a livelihood. You do not learn that you may live – you live that you may learn'.
>
> (John Ruskin, 1869)

Context

Ruskin's words are as relevant today as when they were first written. They are not idealistic but realistic and carry more weight now, particularly with New Labour's emphasis on 'Education, Education, Education' (Blair, 1996) and the 'Learning Society' (Department for Education and Employment (DfEE), 1998). As Freire (1996) argues, for the successful delivery of education, the educators themselves must be able and equipped to deliver. The advent of union learning representatives (ULRs) is a key development in ensuring that this is the case. For the purposes of this book, I have examined the development and growth of the Educational Institute of Scotland's (EIS) Learning Representatives (LRs) against the backdrop of a changing relationship between the key stakeholders in the Scottish education system, particularly since devolution.

This book will show that the EIS LRs are conduits for the continuing professional development (CPD) of teachers and intriguingly are enabling educators to become learners once again as teachers are becoming brokers and facilitators in this process, through taking on the role of being LRs. It is these two factors that may well ensure that Ruskin's words are reality rather than rhetoric.

Before I go any further, I will explain the concept of ULRs and their importance from a Scottish teaching perspective. ULRs are a relatively recent phenomenon and are a new category of lay representation within the workplace in the United Kingdom. They are part of the present New Labour administration's drive to expand and improve lifelong learning and CPD to help create the new *"learning society"* amongst all parts of the British workforce by working in partnership with the trade union movement. This initiative has been given greater credence by the *Employment Act 2002* (Parliament, 2002) which grants a number of statutory rights to ULRs.

The UK is unique in the developed world in that it has established by law that trade unions have the right to not only appoint ULRs but the legislation also allows these representatives paid time-off to train and perform their duties. Of equal significance and unusually in the case of the UK, it has given this right to employees not given in the rest of the European Community, where in many other respects employees have rights denied those in the United Kingdom (Vincenzi and Fairhurst, 2002).

For the purpose of this book, it is important to understand who ULRs are and what their role is. They are trade union lay representatives who receive no financial remuneration apart from expenses accrued in pursuance of their activities. According to the Trades Union Congress (TUC) (2001), anyone can become a learning representative, either by volunteering for the role or being elected by fellow union members. The representatives do not need to have an academic background and many have become ULRs by taking advantage of a learning opportunity, particularly basic skills, computer training and information technology courses (TUC, 2001).

The Scottish Trades Union Congress (STUC) (2005: 6)

which enthusiastically supports this development through its lifelong learning strategy, states that the role of ULRs should encompass the following:

- Establishing and running trade union learning centres
- Negotiating learning agreements with employers, including time off for study
- Helping employees establish employee development schemes
- Monitoring quality of provision
- Raising employee awareness of benefits of learning
- Supporting innovative workplace development, such as SULF [Scottish Union Learning Fund] projects
- Securing equal opportunities in learning
- Providing learning advice and guidance to employees

Grahame Smith the General Secretary of the Scottish Trades Union Congress takes this one step further when he points out that his organisation:

'...strongly supports lifelong learning. Giving workers the opportunity to learn and improve their skills is crucially important to the wellbeing of the individual, employers and the economy of Scotland (STUC, 2007: 3).

ULRs have become significant from the perspective of Scottish teachers due to the recommendations of *The Independent Committee of Inquiry into Professional Conditions of Service of Teachers*, commonly known as the *McCrone Report* that reported in 2000. The report in part dealt with the future of CPD for Scottish teachers. Its chief recommendations in this area were that every teacher should have a personalised CPD plan agreed once a year and any CPD undertaken should be accredited at national level to ensure quality and relevance (McCrone, 2000: 8-9).

To this end the EIS which is the main trade union for teachers in Scotland and represents the overwhelming majority of them, took up the challenge and with the help of a grant from the Scottish Executive (now known as the Scottish Government) launched a LRs initiative with the expressed desire that these representatives work to advise, broker and facilitate improved CPD opportunities for their colleagues (EIS, 2003, Macaulay, 2004, McClintock, 2004).

As I will highlight, the creation of the LRs scheme was a significant development within the Scottish education system from a number of different perspectives. Firstly, it was a significant departure for the EIS as the Institute has created a new tier of lay representatives that cannot be described as typical trade union representatives since they have no bargaining role and no negotiation rights. Secondly, the LRs have moved the EIS from its traditional role as a representative body that dealt in the main with pay and conditions to one that was fully engaged with the learning agenda (Macaulay, 2004). Thirdly, it was one of the first major initiatives by a strategic stakeholder in the Scottish education system in relation to creating a partnership approach to CPD (between the Institute, Scottish Executive, General Teaching Council Scotland (GTCS) and the University of Paisley) based on mutual respect and trust, which was one of the hoped for outcomes of the McCrone Agreement (SEED, 2001).

The book will discuss how the LRs initiative is closely linked to the revitalisation of trade unions through the learning agenda championed by the current New Labour administration (DfEE, 1998). As Sutherland and Rainbird (2000) highlight trade unions such as the EIS have revitalised themselves by actively engaging with the workplace learning initiative and as Wallis et al. (2005) argue unions have gained from the ULR initiative. No more so than with the EIS as I will show as the book progresses.

The Paradigm

My paradigm will be explained in the following paragraphs and expanded upon throughout the book. Denzin and Lincoln (2005: 183) argue that a paradigm highlights a researcher's basic set of beliefs which in turn guided the research process for this study. They point out that a paradigm encompasses the following four terms:

> '...ethics (axiology), epistemology, ontology, and methodology. Ethics ask, "How will I be a moral person in this world?" Epistemology asks "How do I know the world?"...Ontology raises basic questions about the nature of reality and the nature of the human being in the world. Methodology focuses on the best means for acquiring knowledge about the world' (Denzin and Lincoln, 2005:183).

These four terms will act as the book's foundations and guides. My ontological outlook will be explained in greater detail below and it is my intention that the epistemological aspect of the study will run like a red thread throughout the work. Ethics and methodology not only underpinned this study but will be dealt with at greater length in the next chapter.

Ontological Outlook

Etherington (2004: 71) states that:

> 'When I am setting out on any research journey I need to find ways of working that fit with who I am: my underlying values, my philosophies on life, my views of reality and my beliefs about how knowledge is known and created. My view of reality or the nature of being or what is (ontology), and my understanding of what it means to know (epistemology) are intertwined'.

So why should I be writing a book on this subject? On the face of it, there is no compelling reason as I am not a LR; do not work for a recognised trade union and I am a non-active member of the GMB union. As Handy (2001) points out I inhabit the new world of '...elephants and fleas' as I have become one of the growing band of freelancers (fleas) with a '...portfolio career' who work for more than one organisation (elephants) and make their living from more than one source of income. My main area of expertise is human resource management (HRM), which I lecture, research and consult on mainly with the military, police service and international mine-action community.

Thus why am I so attracted to this subject? My answer to this question will be based on two perspectives, personal and professional.

From a personal perspective, I am driven by the experiences and thoughts of my father (Panayis) who was born into abject poverty in Vasili, a small village in Cyprus. Due to his family's dire financial situation, he was denied an education. However, this did not stop him progressing with his life and pursuing his own learning agenda outside formal learning structures as advocated by Freire (1996). In turn, the manner in which he has led his life and his views on the positive aspects of education and learning have guided me.

His outlook and philosophy on life is based on his left-wing political beliefs that centre on the creation of an egalitarian society based on meritocracy, which he believes can in part be achieved by equal access to education and learning opportunities for all. In turn, this is underpinned in his view by the pivotal role of the educator in delivering this (which some would point out is an unrealistic) vision. I always remember as a youngster both my parents (in no small part to their impoverished upbringing) telling my two sisters and I that listening to and obeying the teacher was of the utmost importance in terms of our development. It may seem clichéd and trite to recollect this, but that is the way it was for ethnic families in London and it has stuck for better or worse.

I would argue that my father's beliefs and my parents directions have stimulated not only my own desire for education and learning but also make me believe that the advent of LRs is significant from the perspective of not only developing all of the UK's workforce but also will impact positively on improving the standards and delivery of education to all, particularly children in Scotland.

From a professional perspective, much of my working life has been based around organisations that represent and promote the interests of employees and workplace learning. I have worked for trade unions and representative groups such as the Police Federation of England and Wales, Cranfield University and the Trade Union Research Unit (TURU) based at Ruskin College, Oxford.

It was at Ruskin that I first experienced the positive benefits of post-compulsory education and CPD in the form of a research project that I was heavily involved in with other members of the research team at TURU. This was a long-term project to evaluate the impact of the Ford Employee Development Assistance Programme (EDAP).

The Ford EDAP initiative was set up in 1987 as part of that year's pay and conditions agreement. Its primary aim was to improve the poor industrial relations situation between management and the unions. Relations did improve significantly, but this was a by-product and the key drivers were the opportunity to return to learning, healthier lifestyles and career development. In a nutshell the programme ensures that all Ford employees are eligible for a grant of up to £200 to spend on a course that can either be educational or recreational that will be undertaken on a voluntary basis, in the employee's own time and is distinct and separate from any job-related training that is provided by the company.

The situation in Scotland is similar (although different in many respects) to that of Ford EDAP, in terms of the *McCrone Inquiry* (2000) initially concentrating on pay and terms and conditions but also making significant and far-reaching recommendations regarding CPD and lifelong learning for Scottish teachers. This has had a knock-on effect in stimulating trade union action and employee involvement in terms of the creation of the EIS LRs scheme and it is this connection that has in part stimulated my interest in examining this issue. My participation in the Ford EDAP evaluation left me both fascinated and taken aback by what I witnessed and related to me by participants of the scheme. Employees were genuinely enthused by EDAP and many stated that it had given them a new lease of life, whether it was learning a new language or improving their health by taking up some from of sporting activity.

Thus, my first hand observation of Ford's EDAP scheme is the second key factor in persuading me that the advent of LRs is a positive development and none more so than in the education sector in Scotland. This will be analysed, documented and theorised upon in the remainder of this study.

The Structure of the Book

Taking my lead from Calveley (2005) I will outline my research approach in Chapter 2 as I agree with Calveley (2005: 18) that the reader should share the writer's research journey. I believe that this will give the reader a greater insight not only into how the primary data was collected but also how and why certain arguments and themes develop as the book progresses. The chapter will then focus on the methodological debate surrounding educational research; the ethical implications of this research, particularly how the participants are protected and how their "*voice*" is clearly represented. It also describes the theoretical model adopted for the analysis. The model is based on Ball's (1993) project trajectory studies supported by Bowe et al's. (1992) *context of policy making* model that deals with the contexts of influence, policy text production and practice. By adopting these two approaches, the reader will be able to follow a policy trajectory that begins with policy formulation and its subsequent discourse; how the state responds to it; the introduction and implementation of policy; the interpretation of the policy and its impact on stakeholders and recipients.

Chapter 3 examines the background to the creation of ULRs and outlines the key statutory provisions from a generic perspective. Subsequently, it examines the ULR initiative and learning agenda from a specific Scottish perspective. It follows Ball's (1993) policy trajectory in terms of policy formulation and Bowe et al's. (1992) context of influence and policy text production. This is achieved by examining the McCrone Report (2000); the EIS response to it in terms of creating a LRs scheme and CPD partnerships with key stakeholders; the Scottish Executive stance in relation to the learning agenda and examining the vagaries of the politics of Scottish education with the aim of highlighting the new approach to partnership by the strategic stakeholders in Scottish education.

Chapter 4 discusses the concept of workplace learning and training from a trade union perspective. In so doing it reviews the debate in this field and examines issues such as trade union revitalisation and partnership through the learning agenda and the available academic and practitioner literature in relation to ULRs. It also analyses the discourse in relation to teacher trade union activity from both a collective and individual perspective, concentrating on the debate of how teacher trade unions address the issue of CPD from a representative perspective. This chapter continues to follow Ball's (1993) policy trajectory and Bowe et al's. (1992) context of policy making model by showing the responses to policy formulation, subsequent interpretation and implementation and the impact of this policy on recipients.

Chapter 5 continues to follow Ball's (1993) policy trajectory and Bowe et al's. (1992) context of policy making model by highlighting how the ULRs policy has been interpreted and implemented. This is achieved by examining the views of key stakeholders; the demographic profile of EIS LRs and the support and training they have received from the EIS and the University of Paisley respectively.

Chapter 6 interprets policy and its implementation. It takes both Ball's (1993) and Bowe et al's. (1992) approaches a step further by analysing the impact of the ULRs policy. This is achieved by examining the EIS LRs' relationship with operational stakeholders at both local authority and school level; the obstacles they have faced in relation to carrying out their duties and becoming established and their experiences in dealing with their colleagues.

In Chapter 7, the book moves beyond Ball's (1993) and Bowe et al's (1992) policy trajectory and context of policy making model by exploring the ways forward for the EIS LRs. This is achieved by examining how the LRs have and can develop their role; their perceptions as to how the role will develop in the future and highlights the effect from both a personal and professional perspective of being a LR.

Finally, Chapter 8 brings the book together by highlighting the key issues that have emerged from the analysis. It also builds on Ball's (1993) policy trajectory and Bowe et al's. (1992) context of policy making model by offering observations that the strategic and operational stakeholders within Scottish education can draw upon to refine their learning agenda and the EIS LRs scheme. I also reflect on the research process and its impact at a personal and professional level on myself and speculate on the potential impact on practice.

2

The Research Approach

Introduction

The subject of LRs from an academic perspective is fresh, in that so little has been written about it. My investigation of the literature in relation to this subject indicated there is no theorising about LRs and this gave the study plenty of scope due to the gaps that exist within the literature at both the theoretical and empirical level. It gave me the opportunity to examine teachers as brokers/facilitators of learning for their peers and the impact of LRs to date on the CPD of Scottish teachers. This posed some interesting issues for me as a researcher in terms of my choice of methodology in collating the primary and secondary data for the book and how I sought to theoretically underpin my work.

As outlined earlier, ULRs are a recent phenomenon and as such there is a lack of substantive academic literature analysing and problematisng this new type of union representative. To paraphrase Parkinson (1982: 114) as quoted by Troyna (1994: 1) gaps exist at both the empirical and theoretical level. This chapter will outline the various methodological debates at the theoretical level that informed my research journey.

The Theoretical Discussions

A good starting point is the debate between Ball (1993, 1994) and Henry (1993) on '*what is policy?*'. Ball argues that when analysing complex social issues such as policy it is not advisable to use just one theoretical approach (a position also supported by Hammersley, 2005a) and what is required '...in policy analysis is a toolbox of diverse concepts and theories'. He points out that it is imperative that a researcher understands something thoroughly before they explain it (Ball, 1994: 108).

Further to this Ball (1993: 10) contends that the meaning of policy cannot be taken for granted and if it is to be examined with significant academic rigour much of it will rest '... on the meaning or possible meanings that we give to policy' which in turn affect '..."how" we research and how we interpret what we find'.

In terms of this book the next chapter will explore the LRs from a strategic policy perspective in the form of UK and Scottish government initiatives and legislation that not only seeks to understand how and why LRs came into being but also contextualises it from a Scottish perspective based around the *McCrone Agreement* (SEED, 2001) and how the Scottish Executive, General Teaching Council Scotland (GTCS) and Learning and Teaching Scotland (LTS) have bought into the policy and supported it.

Hammersley (2005a: 140) continues in the same vein as Ball when warning that:

> '...the practice of research cannot be reduced to the following of explicit rules, and that methodological guidance must be developed, in large part, out of actually doing educational research rather than on the basis of preconceived ideas about scientific method'.

Henry (1993: 104) adds to the debate by arguing that policy analysis is:

> '...not only about the workings of policies and their deeper agendas. It is also value-laden activity which explicitly or implicitly makes judgements as to whether and in what ways policies help to "make things better" – acknowledging of course the contested nature of these judgements'.

This ties in with the raison d'être of the EIS LRs to "make things better" for their colleagues in terms of accessing and signing up to Chartered Teacher (CT) in particular. Hammersley (2005b: 8) highlighting the arguments put forward by Edwards (2002) notes the importance of value-laden research and goes on to point out that the '...aim of educational research is to develop educational opportunities and practices', which is one of the objectives of this book.

Ball's (1993) warning dovetails with Kushner's (2000: 80) sound advice that '...Evaluators need to be aware of their beliefs and limitations so as to make more rational methodological choices' and that researchers should not adhere to or support certain methodologies but think of themselves as '... methodologists'.

The debate thus far offers salutary warnings for a researcher, particularly in terms of conduct, values and ethical approach. These three issues will be discussed in greater detail in latter sections of this chapter. In turn they prompted me to adopt a methodology that protected the participants as well as ensuring that their *voice* is clearly heard and runs in parallel with mine rather than being dwarfed or sidelined by it. The data provided by participants is as much theirs as it is mine. As a good friend of mine has highlighted many times, the data the participants provide researchers is a gift and must be treated and respected as one. I hope that this clearly comes across as the book progresses.

The guidance given by Ball (1993, 1994), Hammersley (2005a, 2005b), (Henry 1993) and Kushner (2000) is crucial in forming an understanding as to how to research this subject. This study takes into account the development of the Scottish education system since devolution and the relationship between the key stakeholders in this sector at national and local level as will be outlined in the next chapter. The research also took into account the relationship between the EIS LRs and their local authorities and school managers. The book highlights these key relationships with the aim of ensuring that there is a strong conceptual and theoretical underpinning to this study.

Troyna (1994: 5), argues research such as this cannot be construed as something pristine and must show the researcher grappling '...with the theoretical, ethical and political dramas associated with their research'. Brown and England (2005: 455) take this further by arguing that in research '...failures surely cannot be avoided, and might be understood as healthy components of sincere research enterprises that are designed to provide frameworks from which one can see the world'. I would add that there was a cultural aspect to my research in terms of being an English researcher studying a Scottish initiative. This may well have been to my advantage as I am not involved in the internal politics of the Scottish education system and was distanced from the "centre of the action" geographically. Thus I was as independent as a researcher can get in the circumstances.

Based on the arguments of Hammersley and Atkinson (1983: 209), Troyna (1994: 6) argues that it is of little value for a researcher being reflexive in planning and executing a project if they abandon this approach when writing up the research, a point also highlighted by Etherington (2004). Raab (1994: 18) takes this point further in his discussion of examining educational policy by arguing that policy researchers should move beyond mere description. The book does this, as the review of the academic debate to date shows there has been little conceptualisation, theorising or meaningful discourse on the subject of LRs. Much of the literature can at best be described as descriptive and not substantive.

The book heeds Raab's (1994: 18) warning that to merely describe what is happening can too easily become '...mindless empiricism, contributing relatively little to knowledge and serving no science'.

I took on board the thoughts of Hammersley (1994) based on his discussion centred on ethnographic research, concentrating on the *enlightened paradigm*. This paradigm is based on the relationship between research and practice, where the researcher is able '...to produce the knowledge that is required by policy makers and practitioners, and about the capacity of the knowledge to generate desirable change (Hammersley, 1994: 143), which justifiably can be argued is what the EIS LRs are all about.

In order for this book to have an impact, relevance and value at a conceptual, theoretical and practitioner level, cognisance was taken of Seddon (1996: 197) and her contribution to the debate initiated by Howell (1990) on researchers revealing the '...principle of choice which guides their selection of topics, strategies and resources in policy research'. As this book shows, as a researcher I have nailed my colours to the mast. For example by outlining my ontological approach in the first chapter, that in turn ensured an in-depth examination of policy in practice.

As Seddon (1996: 198-199) highlights it will add to the debate that has arisen about how best to conceptualise the state, policy, power, politics and history, all of which (will be highlighted in the following chapters) are key elements in the construction, formulisation and introduction of LRs within Scottish education and are part of an ongoing discourse and relationship between the key stakeholders in this sector at both the macro and micro level. To this end she argues revealing the *tools* (concepts) of analysis and *toolboxes* (intellectual traditions and communities) as outlined by Ball (1993) will determine how credible and viable my research will be.

Seddon (1996: 199-200) points out that specifying assumptions, concepts, theories and topics; identifying the necessary characteristics of the object of study and elaborating one's own principles will guide the research, in terms of how it is designed, as well as how the evidence will be collected and assessed not only by the researcher themselves but by the intellectual community. In order to grapple with the dilemmas and issues highlighted above, House (1980) points out that there are approaches, standards and principles of evaluation which he splits and labels as either *Objectivist* (i.e. systems analysis approach) and *Subjectivist* (i.e. case study approach) in terms of their epistemology. These factors along with the other key issues discussed thus far informed both the approach and design of the research as will be highlighted in latter sections of this chapter.

I am under no illusion that there are many dangers in terms of my methodological approach and the choices I have made when representing the views and information divulged by persons for this study. However, as House (1980: 254) has highlighted, subjectivist epistemology, particularly the case study approach:

> '...is closely linked to the phenomenological view of man. Contrasted to the view that science alone is the measure of reality and the standard for legitimate knowledge, phenomenologists maintain that one's everyday view of the world, focussing on persons and their behaviour is more fundamental'. Particularly if one thinks of human action, one must think in terms of intentions and of people who guide their behaviour by principles and standards based on community values'.

This is the case in relation to the EIS LRs as the primary research will show and this factor also directed the research design to a great degree. Such thinking fitted in with the type of examination I undertook and guided me, particularly when dealing with the intentions of the EIS LRs in terms of why they volunteered to undertake this role and how they have coped with it.

By the very nature and complexity of the study, it became clear that the theoretical model of analysis to be adopted needed to be based to a lesser or greater degree on what Ball (1993: 16) terms project trajectory studies that:

> '...employ a cross-sectional rather than single level analysis by tracing policy formulation, struggle and response from the state itself through to the various recipients of the policy'.

Because of the natural narrow focus of the book as outlined in the first chapter, Ball's model is used in parts rather than the whole.

Bowe et al.(1992: 19-23) have developed a conceptual framework for this approach based on their *context of a policy making* model. It deals with three contexts all of which are directly relevant to the issues being examined in this book. The contexts are: *the context of influence*, where policy discourses are constructed; *the context of policy text production*, which represents policy and *the context of practice* where policy is not merely received and implemented but interpreted and recreated. The first two contexts will be highlighted and discussed in the next chapter and drove the analysis of the primary data as well as informing the research design.

A key reason for adopting Bowe, Ball and Gold's model concerns the key aspect of all research, that of validity. Stake (2004: 82) is succinct when he argues that '...Probably the greatest weakness of professional evaluation work is the limited validation of interpretations'. Stake (2004: 83) advises that:

> 'It is important for every evaluator to recognize the risk of using unvalidated data-gathering procedures and to caution readers appropriately'.

Brown and England (2005: 449-456) pick up on this dilemma and state that:

> '...the task of research is not to seek truth or to find a final resolution, but rather to ask how the discursive formulations have taken the shape that they have'

and go on to point out that in:

> '...practitioner research the narrative can never catch up with us, but that does not stop us from trying. And our misses can nevertheless be informative. Narratives hold our desires in place even if they do not take us to the place that satisfies them. They can also disrupt our desires and re-educate us about what we want'.

The above debate is taken a step further by Soobrayan (2003: 108) who argues that:

> '...there is no single set of rules or practices that govern the ethics, truth and politics of a research project. However, to guard against the pitfalls of relativism that are implied in this statement, the researcher should recognise that not all statements made in the field can simply be

> accepted as truths and the 'truths' are constantly negotiated and renegotiated in terms of the politics of power in a given context. This does not imply that a laissez faire "anything goes" approach is defensible. On the contrary, the qualitative researcher is consistently called upon to consciously and deliberately engage with the ethical, truth and political implications of his research and writing. For the researcher, ethical epiphanies are rare'.

These important insights were taken on board and have allowed me to ethically and fairly represent participants in this study and be wary of agendas of the persons being researched in terms of the information and knowledge they have imparted. Thus interpreting and representing the views and *voices* of the EIS LRs became a significant ethical factor for this study.

Ethical Considerations

Ethical issues undoubtedly and rightly play a key part in terms of the values that underpin this book as well as the validity of the findings; how I conducted myself; dealt with and treated the participants who volunteered to aid the primary research gathering process. The key issues for this study were how informed consent and trust were gained; how the transfer of information and knowledge pertinent to my research was facilitated and negotiated in a sensitive and respectful manner and represents the participants' views and *voices*. In turn this raised issues such as how their views have been transcribed and related; how and if they should be identified and ensure that they felt free to participate and withdraw from the research process as they saw fit.

The following areas of ethical conduct that I identified were not only relevant and important for this study but time and again in my own previous research and research projects I have been involved in, the issues I highlight in this section have come up. They raised dilemmas and issues that had to be dealt with in order that this book stands up to scrutiny.

On the topic of ethics and research, House (1993: 163) directs researchers to think that '...Ethics are the rules of right conduct or practice, especially the ethical standards of a profession'. Underlying this direction he has put together a set of questions that must be addressed, which I feel are pertinent and relevant to the issues being addressed in this thesis. They are:

- What particular ethical problems do evaluators face?
- What ethical standards have been proposed?
- What general principles underlie these standards?
- Are the standards and principles sufficient to ensure ethical practice?
- What violations of ethics are most likely to occur?

In addition to these questions, I noted with caution the experiences of MacDonald (1976) who identified problems in relation to the portrayal of persons as evaluation data, in particular highlighting persons which will definitely intend to have some consequences for them. This is the case in relation to the EIS LRs as there are relatively few of them and as has been highlighted by Macaulay (2005) everybody knows everybody within the Scottish education sector. This was of concern to me from both an ethical and values perspective but they could not be regarded as vulnerable participants unlike children in educational research (Scott et al., 2006). To deal with this issue, I followed the sound direction of Walford (2005: 84) who states that:

> 'Anonymity is reasonably straightforward. At root, it simply means that we do not name the person or research site involved but, in research, it is usually extended to mean that we do not include information about any individual or research site that will enable that individual or research site to be identified by others'.

There was a distinct possibility that I would encounter obstacles and participants may have sought guarantees as to how their words, views and *voice* are portrayed and some may have wished not to be identified for a variety of disclosed and undisclosed reasons. Some participants may have only participated if the primary data gathering process was undertaken in a certain manner and others may have wished to withdraw because they either felt uncomfortable with the process or compromised.

To deal with expected and unexpected problems, I tackled this issue from a number of angles. Firstly, I adhered to the British Educational Research Association's revised ethical guidelines (BERA, 2004). These guidelines are a good starting point and provide a researcher with a clear and solid direction as to how to conduct themselves as well as how to treat and protect participants in research. They guide researchers as to their responsibilities towards participants; gaining voluntary informed consent; recognising and accepting a participant's right to withdraw from the research without seeking a reason and respecting the privacy of participants by according them the rights of confidentiality and anonymity if requested (BERA, 2004: 4-8). The intention was not only to adhere to these guidelines but to go beyond them and make the participants aware of them by presenting them with a copy of the guidelines.

Secondly, the issue of informed consent was critical in my view to gaining trust and respect. To this end I created a checklist that I referred to throughout the research process. The checklist was in part comprised of the following factors identified by Homan (2002: 24-25) and Miller and Bell (2002: 53):

- It is the requirement that human subjects be informed of the nature and implications of the research and that participation is voluntary.
- Informed consent is a standard principle in a variety of professional practices as well as social research; it is the formulation of a moral obligation to respect others and take account of their interests.
- Consent should be ongoing and renegotiated between the researcher and researched throughout the process.
- Satisfactorily completing an ethics form at the beginning of a study and/or obtaining ethics approval

> does not mean ethical issues can be forgotten, rather ethical considerations should form an ongoing part of the research.

Dealing with informed consent as outlined above added substance to the third part of my approach which was to produce an information sheet for participants involved in the research (akin to the one used by Elliott et al., 2003, in their study of police probationer training and described in some detail by Alexandrou and Davies, 2005) that dealt with the ethics and conduct of the research and acknowledged that all participation was voluntary; all forms of communication would be confidential and respected and no information would be made public that could prove to be detrimental or damaging to a participant and reveal their identity unless I was otherwise informed or instructed by the participants themselves.

Taking this approach one step further, once the cohort of LRs to be researched was identified I introduced myself to them (at one of their regular meetings) and explained the nature and purpose of the research and answered their concerns or queries and gave them verbal assurances as to my intentions and the manner in which I would proceed with the research and my conduct. In addition, I also produced a consent form for the participants to fill in and sign.

As Kushner (1992: 1) states:

> 'Good naturalistic evaluation depends on collaboration rather than just participation; engagement rather than endorsement. Ideally, the evaluator is merely the licensee of the data. But it makes it demanding and intrusive. Being evaluated is not simply being observed. It can be tedious when inaccurate, unsettling and irritating when accurate'.

By adopting this multi-angled approach my aim was not only to protect and respect the participants who volunteered to be part of the research process but also to create a set of standards and criteria by which I and others could measure my behaviour as a researcher.

Research Design and Methods

Greckhamer and Koro-Ljunberg (2005: 735) point out that '...Research methods refer to the concrete techniques or procedures the researcher engages in to gather and analyze data' and for this study there was a need to carefully evaluate the methods to be utilised.

The methods adopted needed to complement each other in this mixed-methods approach (Phillips, 2004). Taking into account the previous discussion on the choice of analytical framework and ethical approach, the subject of this research in the main lent itself to a qualitative approach in terms of data collection with some quantitative analysis based on a preliminary questionnaire.

The quantitative approach as Weiss (1998: 82-84) points out allows the researcher to collect objective data but also to identify relationships amongst variables and reach conclusions with a '...known degree of confidence about the distribution of the phenomenon'.

However, I felt it was imperative to engage participants on a personal basis through the use of loosely semi-structured or unstructured interviews; the writing of personal records; question and answer sessions and ad-hoc consultation groups; a telephone survey and observation. All qualitative techniques highlighted by Weiss (1998: 82) that I believed would add to my understanding of the issues (rather than produce further precise measurements) and ensured a research process that evolved and was flexible based on the analysis of the data and knowledge gained (Weiss, 1998: 82-83).

Weiss (1998: 86) argues that the use of qualitative methods are:

> '...usually superior for capturing processes that nobody thought of measuring at the beginning, for understanding the meaning of program processes to people in different positions, and for finding unexpected patterns of association in unexpected data'.

Thus a case study approach was adopted because of the access given to me by the EIS; the time-frame of the research and the flexibility it allows a researcher to gather data from a number of different sources using a number of different approaches. As Weiss (1998: 261) highlights in terms of adopting the case study approach:

> '...it is hard to think of a case study as a particular design...It tries to consider interrelationships among people, institutions, events and beliefs. Rather than breaking them down into separate items of analysis, the case study seeks to keep all elements of the situation in sight at once'.

Stake (2005: 449-450) takes this a step further when he argues that a researcher should place their:

> '...best intellect into the thick of what is going on. The brainwork ostensibly is observational, but more critically, it is reflective. In being ever-reflective, the researcher is committed to pondering the impressions, deliberating on recollections and records – but not necessarily following the conceptualizations of theorists, actors, or audiences'.

Taking the above into consideration and that this piece of research is underpinned by the Democratic Evaluation approach to educational research, where the voice of the participant is primary (House, 1993, Kushner, 2000, Stake, 2004) a number of different methods were used to gather and disseminate the data. Firstly, background information was collected from key policy documents and academic literature. Secondly, national officials of the EIS and other Scottish education stakeholders were either interviewed personally, by e-mail or provided a personal written record in order to give me background, context and views as to the current situation and future of the Institute's LRs initiative. Thirdly, the first group of LRs (31 in total) was asked to participate in the research by filling in a questionnaire; writing a personal record of their experiences to date; participating in consultation forums and question and answer sessions at their regular LR meetings. Finally, these findings were backed up by a short telephone survey of head teachers.

The interviews were based on either a semi-structured or unstructured approach and participants were free to answer as many or as few of the questions that were put to them. They also had the opportunity to determine where and how the interview took place. The majority of the interviews were face-to-face in either the participants' working environment; home or hotel. One interview was conducted through e-mail correspondence due to lack of time on the part of the participant and one participant was not only happy to be interviewed but also produced a personal record.

As stated above this book focuses on the first group of 31 LRs, as at the time they were already in place and it was a feasible number to examine in-depth. In terms of the questionnaire, the participants were asked to give demographic details as well as answering questions as to why they chose to become an LR; their relationship with their own institution on becoming an LR; their experiences and relationship with their respective local authorities and school CPD advisers; obstacles they have faced in undertaking their roles and responsibilities as an LR; their experiences in dealing with their colleagues as well as a number of other issues

In relation to the personal records, the participants were asked to volunteer to write them and were informed that not all of them were expected to participate in this phase of the research They were asked to consider a number of issues (some of which had been dealt with in the questionnaire) and as a guide I produced a list to help them structure the focus of their responses. Participants were also encouraged to write on any issue they felt was important. However, most focused on the list of the issues I produced.

I felt that in order to build upon the data collected from the questionnaire, and to ensure that the voice of the participants clearly came through in the research process, writing a personal record was the best approach as with more time on their side, participants would be able to deliberate for longer and deeper about the issues surrounding their roles as LRs, which would not be the case if they were to be interviewed.

In addition to the questionnaires and personal records, the LRs at their quarterly meetings participated in question and answer sessions and ad-hoc consultation groups with me. This method allowed me to continually update my knowledge of how the LRs were progressing and what issues they were currently facing.

In turn this data was further supplemented by a short telephone survey of head teachers that sought to deal with certain issues highlighted by the interviewees and the LRs. Participants for this telephone survey were randomly selected from a database of head teachers kept by the EIS with the aim of trying to cover all 32 local authority areas. By the end of the process 16 primary heads and 16 secondary heads were selected and this cohort covered 27 of the local authority areas. The participants were contacted by letter in advance of the phone call to ask them to participate in the research. In order to keep the research "clean", the participants were not told specifically what the survey was about but informed it was about investigating aspects of the EIS' professional role. The aim was not to give advance notice thus rendering the results skewed and unusable. Many consented to participate either by calling, e-mailing or accepting on the day of the call.

In total thirty one questionnaires were distributed and twenty nine were returned, a 93.5% response rate. Fourteen (45.2%) of the participants agreed to write a personal record and 32 head teachers were contacted for the telephone survey with 31 (96.9%) responding. Such a significant response to the main phase of the primary research process indicates that, not only are this cohort of LRs committed to the whole concept of this type of representation but they also along with the other participants had faith in the research process, which in turn helped to validate the research data.

The research approach outlined above can be described as interrogating the data with data (Kushner, 2000) with the aim of ensuring the validity of the research process and to triangulate the primary research data. This in turn ensures that the findings, conclusions and recommendations stand up to scrutiny (House, 1980).

The next chapter will firstly, examine the background to the creation of ULRs and secondly, highlight how this policy has been interpreted and implemented from a specific Scottish perspective. It aims to highlight what Ball (1993) terms policy formulation and Bowe et al's (1992) context of influence and policy text production in relation to LRs as well as highlighting the beginning of the context of practice where policy is being interpreted and represented.

3

Background to the Creation of Learning Representatives and the Scottish Perspective

Introduction

This chapter examines how and why ULRs came into being in terms of policy initiatives, statutory recognition and related rights. It will also examine how this policy has been interpreted in Scotland by analysing the strategic stakeholders' responses from a CPD and partnership perspective within the political context of Scottish education.

The Initiatives Leading to the Creation of ULRs

The creation of ULRs can be traced to several significant initiatives that have been launched by the present New Labour administration. The first was the establishment of the National Advisory Group for Continuing Education and Lifelong Learning (Nagcell) in 1997, chaired by Professor R.H. Fryer and with the express remit of advising the Secretary of State for the Department for Education and Employment (DfEE) (as it was then named) on matters concerning adult learning (Fryer,1997). In its first report Nagcell asserted that the:

> '...active involvement of trade unions will assist in legitimising the purposes and processes of workplace learning in the eyes of their members facilitating take up of learning and the development of learning partnerships at work'. (Fryer, 1997: Para.10.16).

The second of these initiatives was the creation of the *Union Learning Fund* (ULF) for trade unions announced in *The Learning Age* Green Paper (DfEE, 1998), followed by the Scottish Executive setting up the Scottish Union Learning Fund (SULF) in 2000 (STUC, 2005: 3). As The National Literacy

Trust (2003) and the Labour Research Department (LRD) (2001) both note, the ULF was established as part of the DfEE's strategy to encourage a culture of lifelong learning through developing workplace initiatives and boost unions' capacity as learning organisations, as outlined by Nagcell in its first report and highlighted above.

The Department for Education and Skills (DfES) (2002:4) noted that the ULF helped to pave the way for the introduction and development of ULRs and to establish a nationwide network of trained learning representatives, which could rise to over 22,000 by 2010. The STUC (2005: 3) adds to this by pointing out that in:

> '...the first round of the Scottish Union Learning Fund, 12 projects were approved and many of these looked to build an increased capacity with the union to promote learning in the workplace. Central to this was the development of the role of the Union Learning Representative – a new form of activist who would become the major focus for driving learning activity within trade unions at local level'.

The third initiative was the 1998 report of the TUC Learning Services Task Group (TUC, 1998). It dealt with a range of vocational and other learning issues that concerned trade unions and their members. Significantly, it called for the development of a network of ULRs who would be backed up by trade union support in terms of campaigning and highlighting their role; creating information and support structures; setting standards for and training them and campaigning for them to have statutory rights (TUC, 1998: 221-222). The statutory recognition aspect was pursued with much vigour by the TUC, based on the success of the ULF and SULF projects that recruited and trained many ULRs. This was highlighted by the TUC and the STUC and in turn had a significant effect on the Government (Clough, 2006).

It led to the fourth initiative in the form of the *Learning to*

Succeed White Paper (DfEE, 1999) which had the principle aim of opening up the debate in terms of creating a new framework for post-16 learning. It recognised that trade unions had a role to play and it shows some joined up thinking by the Government with regard to the ULF and ULRs. It argued that: '...The Union Learning Fund is playing a key part in developing a network of Learner Representatives' (DfEE, 1999:66).

Further credence and authority was given to both the unions and the ULRs in the Department for Trade and Industry (DTI) and the DfEE White Paper entitled *Opportunity for All in a World of Change* (2001) which stated:

> 'We are committed as a Government to ensuring that Union Learning Representatives can play their part in both the competitiveness of the enterprise and the personal investment and gains for the employee for lifelong learning' (DTI and DfEE, 2001: Para. 2.42).

The White Paper proposed to give statutory backing to ULRs (DTI and DfEE, 2001: Para.2.42). As John Monks (then General Secretary of the TUC) pointed out, education and learning have been core elements of trade union and TUC business and ever since the TUC's inception, '...there has been a continuing belief that improving skills will improve opportunities for union members'. He argues that there has been a *"Quiet Revolution"* since 1998 with the introduction, development and growth of ULRs (TUC, 2001).

Statutory Rights for ULRs

Following the publication of the White Paper (DTI and DfEE, 2001), the Government set about giving ULRs greater credence and statutory recognition and was achieved with the enactment of the *Employment Act 2002.* This legislation put ULRs on a statutory footing (as of April 2003) and not only does it give recognised trade unions the right to appoint learning representatives it also allows ULRs to have paid leave to perform their duties (Section 43 (1)). Section 43 (2) of the

Act sets out the activities of the representatives as: analysing learning or training needs, providing information and advice on learning and training matters, arranging learning or training and promoting their value. The legislation also requires ULRs to be trained and to be entitled to reasonable time-off to undertake their duties. The amount of time itself must relate directly to the representatives' activities (Section 43 (3-6)).

The statutory recognition is given further credence and teeth in that it is accompanied by a code of practice on time-off for trade union activities, which specifically includes guidance on time-off for learning representatives (Advisory, Conciliation and Arbitration Service (ACAS), 2003). It reinforces the provisions of the Act, clarifies issues and gives specific direction to ULRs. For example, the code highlights that many employers already have in place well established employee training and development programmes and directs learning representatives to liaise with employers to ensure that their respective training activities complement rather than duplicate each other (ACAS, 2003:10).

The Scottish Perspective

Anderson (2003: 219) states that:

> 'Scottish education has been characterised by a peculiar awareness of its own history. Since 1707 its distinctness has been a mark of national identity to be defended against assimilation with England, and its supposed superiority has been a point of national pride. Two achievements were especially notable: the early arrival of universal or near-universal literacy, and a precociously developed university system'.

In addition, McPherson and Raab (1988: 29) point out that the '...government of education in Scotland' is based on centralisation and partnership

The three pillars of distinctness, centralised control and partnership impact on the professional development of Scottish teachers which as Purdon (2003: 942) argues has changed considerably in the past seven years and that 2000 has '... proved to be a particularly significant year in terms of CPD for teachers', as the Standards in Schools Act 2000 (the first to be passed by the newly created Scottish Parliament) extended the GTCS's remit in relation to the career development of Scottish teachers. Whilst, the importance attached to their CPD was further enhanced by recommendations made in the McCrone Report (2000) which were briefly mentioned in the previous chapter and will be highlighted in greater detail below.

The remainder of the chapter will introduce the EIS; how the Scottish Executive has tackled the issue of lifelong learning and the EIS response to the challenges thrown up by the *McCrone Agreement* (Scottish Executive Education Department (SEED), 2001) and the challenges laid down by the Scottish Executive.

The Educational Institute of Scotland

Official figures show that the Scottish teaching profession is extensively unionised and the EIS is the largest teaching union in Scotland (Certification Officer, 2007:72). The EIS was officially formed in 1847 and in Belford's (1946: 63) history of the EIS, celebrating the Institute's centenary, he states that:

> '...not merely for mutual benefit did these teachers associate; believing in the worth of human personality, they wished to proclaim the necessity for education and establish the value of sound learning'.

The Institute was further strengthened when in 1851, it was granted its first Royal Charter, with the guiding principle of the Charter being the upholding of educational standards (Belford, 1946: 327-334).

Thus the foundation stones were laid not only for the EIS as a representative body but as an organisation that would seek to put the education of the populace at the core of its mission and invest in the CPD of its members. This tradition seems to have been maintained to this day by the Institute's response to the challenges laid down by the *McCrone Report* (2000), in relation to teacher CPD and its investment in its LRs.

Currently, the EIS has approximately 59,000 members, which equates to representing 80% of teachers in Scotland, covering the nursery, primary, secondary and special education sectors, as well as representing lecturers in further and higher education and as the '...oldest teaching union in the world' reaffirms its guiding principles by stating it '...has a firm commitment to quality education provision for all young people' (EIS, 2007, Macaulay and Maclean, 2006).

The McCrone Report

An independent committee of inquiry into the pay and conditions of service for Scottish teachers, headed by Professor Gavin McCrone, was set up by the then Minister for Children and Education, Sam Gailbraith. This was in response to the breakdown in negotiations over pay and conditions between the employers and unions in 1999 (McCrone, 2000:1). Its terms of reference were primarily to examine:

> '...how teachers' pay, promotion structures and conditions of service should be changed in order to ensure a committed, professional and flexible teaching force which will secure high and improving standards of school for all children in Scotland into the new millennium...'

and the inquiry team was encouraged to make recommendations based on a number of principles (McCrone, 2000:71), although not one of them dealt explicitly with the issue of CPD.

However, the final report made a number of recommendations that would impact on the issues of CPD and teacher status that would lead the EIS to take on board the concept of LRs.

In relation to CPD the report made the following recommendations:

> 'Courses offered under the heading of CPD should be accredited at national level to ensure their quality and

relevance.

Local authorities should review their arrangements for the provision of organised CPD activity in their region to assess its effectiveness.

The Scottish Executive should establish a national register of approved CPD providers, and review the financing available to schools to support CPD activity.

Every teacher should have an individual CPD plan agreed once a year with his or her immediate manager.

All primary and secondary schools who have not yet done so should designate a CPD co-ordinator from among the teaching staff to facilitate the management of CPD in the school. For smaller schools, a co-ordinator could be designated for each cluster.

In view of the importance of CPD, local authorities should, in consultation with the teaching unions, increase time available for professional development by the equivalent of a further five days a year. This may be undertaken flexibly either outwith the school day or outside the pupil year. This additional commitment should be reflected in the salary structure' (McCrone, 2000: 63-64).

The inquiry team made a number of recommendations in relation to career structures, most notably:

'…In order to recognise and reward excellence in the classroom and encourage continuing professional development within the teaching profession, the Committee also recommends that the Scottish Executive, together with the GTC and TEIs and consulting local authority employers and the teaching unions, should develop by the end of the year a national programme and standards for Chartered Teacher status to be implemented by 1 April 2002. This programme should be open to all experienced classroom teachers. The Committee expects Chartered Teacher status to be within reach of a significant majority of teachers; and anticipates that they would be motivated to achieve it. It would constitute a personal achievement, rather than a post'

In relation to Chartered Teacher (CT), the Committee stated that it would be necessary to develop a programme which involves:

> '...attestation through the annual review process of high standards of teaching and professionalism, subject to external moderation to ensure consistent application across Scotland; it would require completion of a challenging and structured programme of relevant and accredited CPD, over a period of four years, aimed at improving teaching and other professional skills. In the early years of the scheme, consideration should be given to the practicality of a fast-track procedure for teachers already at the top of the scale and who have already undertaken significant amounts of CPD, subject to validation.
>
> Progress towards, and achievement of, Chartered Teacher status would be rewarded with additional salary points. Once acquired, teachers would keep the status and the associated salary points if they transferred to another school. Acquisition of Chartered Teacher status would not involve taking on any additional management responsibility beyond that of a main grade teacher. We would, however, expect that Chartered Teachers would play an important part as role models for junior colleagues. In the Committee's view, such a chartering scheme should provide an attractive option for teachers who do not wish to seek promotion to middle management but to develop their classroom skills through CPD' (McCrone, 2000: 20-21).

In the spirit of partnership, all the key stakeholders in Scottish education agreed to the recommendations (commonly referred to as the *McCrone* Agreement (SEED, 2001)) and the uniqueness that was highlighted earlier is trumpeted in the introduction to this agreement which states that the:

> '...areas of agreement and the detail covered have been achieved through a unique process of discussion and dialogue among employers, teacher representatives and the Scottish Executive...We have agreed that, for the future, the working relationships between teacher organisations, employers and the Scottish Executive will be based on mutual respect and understanding, on shared responsibility and on the shared development of ideas and programmes for change (SEED, 2001: 2).

The key factor to consider in relation to the above statements is that this is fine rhetoric but what is the reality in terms of the LRs and can the partnership approach work when there are a number of agendas being pursued by the various stakeholders?

The Scottish Executive's Stance on Lifelong Learning

The Scottish Executive has not been slow in taking up the mantle of championing lifelong learning and has been involved in a number of initiatives and publication of reports that have underlined its commitment to this issue. As Fairley (2003: 133) points out (quoting the Enterprise and Lifelong Department [ELLD, 2001: 3]) it has also '...adopted a definition of lifelong learning as: "the continuous development of the skills, knowledge and understanding that are essential for employability and personal fulfilment"'. In turn these have had a direct impact on the EIS LR scheme as the following short chronology of initiatives and publications will show.

In 1998, the Department for Education and Science (DES) set out it vision for lifelong learning in Scotland for the period 1998-2002 in *Opportunity for Scotland* (Scottish Office, 1998). Fairley (2003: 133) identified the five key themes of this document as '...raising awareness; improving access; extending participation; encouraging progress; ensuring quality'. This was followed in 1999 by a consultation paper on training at work entitled *Developing Skills and Employability* (Scottish Office,

1999) and in 2000 the SULF was established (STUC, 2005). In 2001, the Scottish Parliament's Enterprise and Lifelong Learning Committee set up an Inquiry into Lifelong Learning and reported in 2002, with the key recommendation that the Scottish Executive should develop a lifelong learning strategy. It also identified six areas that required changes in terms of providing learning for the future and these were demographic, economic, social justice, citizenship, skill shortages and technological (Scottish Parliament, 2002).

The following year, the Scottish Executive set out its five-year lifelong learning strategy entitled *Life Through Learning; Learning Through Life*. In the forward to this document Iain Gray, the then Minister for Enterprise, Transport and Lifelong Learning stated that: '...We want people to be motivated to expand their learning and develop their skills and be enterprising in their attitudes to work' (Scottish Executive, 2003: 4-5).

The strategy has what it terms five *people centred goals*, with the two key goals being:

> '...A Scotland where people's knowledge and skills are recognised, used and developed to best effect in their workplace...
>
> A Scotland where people are given the information, guidance and support they need to make effective learning decisions and transitions' (Scottish Executive, 2003: 6).

As the strategy is outlined above the EIS LRs should in theory be able to play a significant role in helping the Executive deliver this strategy within the Scottish education sector. This assumption is backed up to a degree by the strategy stating that trade unions as stakeholders:

> '...have a key role to play in workforce development through influencing employers to provide training and employees to take up the opportunities. They also play an important role in providing learning themselves and leading workplace learning projects' (Scottish Executive, 2003:13).

This is clearly the case with the EIS and its LR initiative as will be demonstrated below. It is also another example of not only the partnership approach being pushed forward as a means of moving the lifelong learning agenda forward but also the unique and distinct manner that it can be achieved by the stakeholders within the Scottish education sector. This was recently backed up by then Deputy Minister for Enterprise and Lifelong Learning, Allan Wilson, who stated that:

> '...Skills, education and lifelong learning continue to be key to the government agenda. They are also at the heart of the union movement...Unions and Union Learning Representative (ULRs) need to work in partnership with employers if we are to get members switched on to learning again. We need to be in the workplace with a strong learning message...We know we face a challenge. And, in ULRs, we have the people to meet the challenge. Don't underestimate yourselves. Your enthusiasm and drive makes a difference. It is your positive example that inspires others to learn. It is your commitment to learning that makes others committed' (STUC, 2007: 5-6).

The EIS Response

Following the McCrone Inquiry's (2000) damning attack on the inadequacy of CPD provision, the EIS took some positive action and this was based on a two-pronged approach. The first aspect of its response dealt with CPD and it entered into a partnership with the University of Paisley to provide CPD courses for its members. To date it has developed a Diploma Programme with eight modules that allows teachers to be awarded not only the GTCS certificate for achieving CT status but an academic qualification from the University of Paisley that could lead to the award of a Masters degree by continuing their studies. It is also developing with the LTS a Certificate and Diploma programme with the specified aim of teachers developing their subject specific skills (EIS, 2003, Macaulay,

2004). This approach fits in with the stated aim of the *McCrone Agreement* (SEED, 2001) that the stakeholders should work in partnership and again highlights the distinct and unique nature in which this can be achieved. It also fits in with the stated aims and ethos of the Institute but it is the second aspect of its approach that saw it taking a step into the unknown in terms of introducing a new initiative that the EIS admits is "… a culture shock" (Macaulay, 2004).

The EIS felt that it was not enough just to enter into a partnership with the University of Paisley to develop and implement CPD programmes for teachers. It felt that it needed to underpin this initiative with a level of support unprecedented in its history to date and it applied to the SULF via the ELLD of the Scottish Executive for a grant to set up a learning representatives scheme (Macaulay, 2004).

In its bid submission the Institute stated that:

> 'The development of teacher CPD, led by the Scottish Executive Education Department (in consultation with stakeholders including the EIS) articulates well with the five "people centred goals" identified in the Lifelong Learning Strategy for Scotland published in February 2003. In particular the EIS shares the Scottish Executive's aims for a "high quality learning experience" available to teachers; ensuring teachers' "knowledge and skills are recognised, used and developed to best effect in their workplace". Most notably the development of the Learning Representative programme within the EIS would help ensure that teachers are "given the information, guidance and support they need to make effective decisions and transitions"' (EIS, 2003).

Macaulay (2004) explained that the initial aim of the EIS was to try and identify and appoint LRs to help with its CPD initiatives but it got knocked back in its bid for self-funding to take the project forward. However, the Institute was encouraged to put a bid in with the Department for Education (whose civil servants were pro-active on this issue) and it agreed to give funding to the EIS for basically the same proposal it had put in to the other department. The funding was significantly less then the original amount requested as it would not fund the element of the bid that dealt with LR development with the University of Paisley. What the Department agreed to fund was the capacity building of LRs within the Institute's structures. This initiative was another sign of the partnership approach and as will be shown below will again highlight the distinct and unique way in which the EIS and other stakeholders are tackling the CPD issue through LRs.

Macaulay (2004) describes how the EIS set the wheels in motion by creating a Masters level module that would train the new LRs and would be of a significantly higher academic standard then the TUC/STUC ULR course. He states that the module is demanding and based around lifelong learning delivered through e-learning. It is a notional 150 hours module with the criteria for the course having been developed by the University. There is formal recognition by Paisley and in addition the EIS has developed its own certificate for this course. The module is not only accredited by the University it is also supported by the EIS' other partners in its CPD/LR initiative including the Scottish Executive. This is a unique and distinct approach based on the partnership principle as all the other unions who have put in place LRs have used the TUC/STUC course. Significantly, in addition to this unique approach the EIS has ensured a permanent full-time post is also part of this project and Lyn McClintock was appointed to the post in November 2003 with a specific remit to look after the LRs and associated CPD initiatives. This post was partially funded from the grant from the Department and since March 2005, the EIS has taken over the funding of it.

Macaulay (2004) explained that the initial objective of the Institute was to have 50 LRs within its 32 Local Associations (which mirror the number of local authorities in Scotland). At the time of the research, the EIS had 31 LRs in place but its long-term aim is to have in place one LR in each of Scotland's 3,500 schools.

Macaulay (2004) also explained that the EIS has a number of Further Education (FE) LRs who have attended the TUC/STUC course but the Institute's ambition is to bring together all its LRs to work in one cohesive unit. He went on to elaborate that another desired aim is to have two tiers of LRs. One group will work with local authorities and the other group at establishment level.

McClintock (2004, 2005) stated that the first tranche of LRs had successfully completed their course and been accredited between September 2003 and June 2004 and are now fully established. She pointed out that since her appointment not only has she been overseeing the implementation of the LR initiative, but has also given local association secretaries assistance, information and support in the negotiations for time-off for the representatives with their respective local authorities.

For the purposes of this book, the first tranche of 31 LRs were evaluated, as they were already in place and it was a feasible number to examine in-depth.

The Politics of Scottish Education

McPherson and Raab (1988: x-xi) in their seminal work discussing the governance of Scottish education between 1945-1987 state that 'Scottish educational policy has been made by its own cast of characters, in its own setting and, for the most part, with its own scripts' and that they found two emergent themes, expansion and partnership. As previously indicated in this chapter, this is still the case in the post-devolution era, particularly in relation to lifelong learning. What is also clear from their text is that the Scottish educational system is a close-knit community, where it seems everyone knows everyone else. As they point out throughout their work, there have been conflicts as well as agreement and that: 'Educational issues were explicitly discussed in terms of their implications for social solidarity and social mobility, for a traditional and open community on the one hand, and for a nationally efficient society on the other' (McPherson and Raab, 1988: 50).

However, as Allan (2003: 290) based in part on the arguments of Bryce and Humes (1999) points out that before devolution '...educational policymaking in Scotland was directed by the Scottish Education Department and...has been centralized, consensual and orthodox. Dissenting voices are marginalized and strategies of containment limit the flow of information and create a conformist ideology in which discussion is restricted to procedural matters'. It seems that this situation has changed since devolution as has been previously highlighted.

Johnston and MacKenzie (2003: 86-97) show that since devolution, there has been a radical change in the political structures that govern Scottish education that seem to encourage more discourse between stakeholders but also more accountability to the Scottish people by politicians and civil servants. It can be argued that this greater openness from the politicians has allowed stakeholders such as the EIS to be bold with such initiatives as its LRs initiative but has to be tempered by the fact that tensions exist between the stakeholders who will all naturally have their separate agendas. As Kirk (2000: 16) points out, the '...education of teachers is an area of public policy that is not short of stakeholders' and how '...are the claims of these various stakeholders to be reconciled?'. He goes on to state that:

> '...new forms of continuing professional development for teachers are creating opportunities for the intensification of collaborative activities and for the emergence of ways of working that fully justify the term partnership' (Kirk, 2000: 34).

This is clearly the case with the EIS LRs and one in which the internecine politics of Scottish education will have a significant bearing on.

Humes (2003: 77-79) picks up on the themes outlined above

by pointing out the indications are that there is '... a strong political commitment to the importance of education in post-devolution Scotland' based for example on the *McCrone Inquiry* and its subsequent recommendations; the expansion of the role of the GTCS and the Scottish Executive having to '...justify policy decisions on the basis of the contribution they would make to the improvement of quality in education'. This has been indicated in the previous sections of this chapter with the official pronouncements in relation of lifelong learning.

He goes on to argue that it is no longer sensible to argue that there is one single policy community within Scottish education and that:

> '...it might be more meaningful to refer to a number of over overlapping policy communities, rather than a single coherent entity. Thus it might make sense to speak of a range of policy communities each with a particular focus...There will be points of convergence between these but, for many purposes they will remain separate'(Humes, 2003:83).

The evidence presented in this chapter suggests that this is the case in relation to LRs and that there is a specific LRs/CPD policy community. The book will examine the interrelationship of the stakeholders within this policy community and how it affects the manner in which LRs operate.

Paterson (2000: 1) states that:

> 'Education cannot help being at the centre of the concerns of the Scottish Parliament. For over a century, now, there has been a strengthening belief that a parliament could make better policy for education than the unreformed union has managed, and could link that efficiently to social needs'.

For example, the EIS LRs scheme has been developed from the Parliament's significant interest in teacher CPD and lifelong learning.

On a similar theme Alexiadou and Ozga (2002: 685-686)

contentiously point out that since devolution there is the '...emerging centrality of the Scottish Parliament' in terms of Scottish education that has:

> '...obvious implications for issues that tell us about changing governance, for example, in relation to the role of local government and to the place of the teaching profession in policy-making'.

This is central to the issues that will be examined in this book as the teaching profession in the form of the EIS is significantly involved in the policy process and its subsequent implementation in relation to teacher CPD as evidenced by its LRs initiative and its partnership with the University of Paisley.

Paterson (2000: 34) takes this a step further by arguing that greater interaction amongst the stakeholders is driven by the Scottish Parliament and '...widespread consultation will ensure that policy is better implemented because teachers and others will be less sceptical about it'. This study will seek to establish whether this assumption is valid or whether the tensions that led to the *McCrone Inquiry* still exist, particularly as Menter et al. (2004: 202) argue that if:

> '...teacher development policy [in Scotland] is to have a significance beyond narrow questions of conditions, pay and progression, then the overall value system within which the framework is to be located needs to be spelt out'.

In terms of the EIS LRs this will impact on the relationship between the various stakeholders and is unavoidably intertwined in the politics of Scottish education as Menter et al. (2004: 203) indicate by highlighting that McCrone attacked the existing power relationships in Scottish education that had led to his Inquiry being set up.

Paterson (2005: 1) in his discussion on the dilemmas of education and democracy takes this discussion of the politics of Scottish education to a new level by arguing that with the decline of the authority and influence of such social bastions as the church, traditional community organisations and politicians:

> '...it may be that the teacher is now, in many communities, the only person who can carry the weight of ethical and even political leadership'.

If this is to be the case, then their professional development is inextricably linked to this proposition and the role of LRs will be significant.

The next chapter reviews the debate relating to LRs, workplace learning and training from a trade union perspective and trade union representation amongst teachers. The analysis further contextualises the key issues being examined in this book and also continues to follow Ball's (1993) policy trajectory and Bowe et al's. (1992) context of policy making model showing the responses to policy formulation; subsequent interpretation and implementation and the impact of this policy on recipients.

4

Unions and the Learning Debate

Introduction

The debate in relation to ULRs is emergent. There are a number of independent reports and publications produced by both the academic and practitioner communities and these will be discussed in detail in this chapter.

For the purposes of this study, the review of the debate thus far will be split into three distinct areas. The first area will examine workplace learning and training from a trade union perspective. It will act as the basis of the chapter and lead into and underpin the debate that directly pertains to ULRs, which will be the substantive element of this chapter. The final area will be an examination of the discourse in relation to teacher trade union activity from both a collective and individual level. These three areas are interconnected and throughout the book key themes that have been identified from these various strands of the debate will be linked and will help to further underpin the conceptual and theoretical aspects of this book.

Workplace Learning and Training from a Trade Union Perspective

Dehmel (2005:7) in her discussion on the role of vocational education and training in promoting lifelong training points out that it has '…increasingly emerged as a key focus at national as well as international levels' and I would contend none more so than for the trade union movement based on the policy initiatives highlighted in the previous chapters. As Forrester (2004: 418-419) points out:

> 'For trade unions, the workplace will always remain the primary focus of learning and attention…There can

> be little doubt that recent union activities on workplace learning, such as the creation of a network of union learning representatives and the promotion of lifelong learning, marks an important and significant development in the search for relevance in today's world of work'.

Rainbird (2000:10) highlights the conflictual nature of learning within the workplace, which in turn impacts both on trade unions and their members in terms of how they deal with this issue. Rainbird et al. (2004: 52) add to this by arguing that:

> '...consensus and participation have to be constructed as a means of facilitating learning on the basis of recognizing the different and opposing interests of workers and employers, rather than taken as a given'.

These observations fit in with the situation faced by the EIS LRs, as they are helping to implement the *McCrone Agreement* and as Rainbird (2000:10) states we must at all times bear in mind who initiates and who benefits from workplace learning. This is what this book is in part trying to discover. Particularly, as Rainbird (2000:10) goes on to argue that unions '...owe it to their members to retain critical appreciation of where their interests lie' and they '...need to formulate strategies towards the work modernisation agenda which encompass workplace learning'. In a nutshell this is what is happening in the Scottish education sector as a result not only of the *McCrone Agreement* but also the EIS' response to it through its LRs and CPD initiatives.

Sutherland and Rainbird (2000: 189-209) take the discussion further when they ask if unions should be in conflict with or cooperate with employers over workplace learning. As they point out the European Union (EU) has:

> '...been instrumental in encouraging the use of collective agreements on continuing vocational training as a means of promoting social dialogue on training'.

They go on to state that the '...lifelong learning agenda opens up new opportunities for trade unions to develop strategies towards workplace learning' and proceed to argue that unions are interested in workplace learning firstly, so members can, '...enhance their employability and bargaining', secondly, '...in some instances, members are employed in educational institutions as teachers' and thirdly, '...there are broader citizenship issues which trade unionists need to address as members of society and parents' (Sutherland and Rainbird, 2000: 191-193). These points again have cognisance with the issues being examined in this study.

Forrester and Payne (1999, 2000), Forrester (2001) and Payne (2001) should be credited with being the first to highlight the role of ULRs in the workplace from an academic perspective but their work stems in the main from considering the issue of trade unions and workplace learning and training. Forrester (2001: 318) argues that:

> 'Trade union education...has tended to mirror the wider fortunes and complexities both within the particular union (or unions) and within the socio-economic environment'.

Whilst Payne (2001) asks '*What do trade unions want from lifelong learning?*'. This question is in part answered by Haunch and Bennett (2002:3) in their paper that deals with learning partnerships and ULRs. They argue that it:

> '...has long been recognised that unions in the UK have accepted the need to embrace new learning in the workplace...Furthermore, increasingly, training and development and lifelong learning are becoming a more general focus of union activity nationally, and more specifically in the workplace. Critically, developing learning opportunities is seen as a key strategy for retaining and enhancing union membership'.

Sutherland and Rainbird (2000:195) add to this debate by arguing that unions need to develop a strategy towards workplace learning based on the following questions:

'...should the initiation of learning strategies be left to management? Should trade unionists simply add learning opportunities to the list of periodic demands in the context of traditional collective bargaining and the annual pay round? If not, what might the role of trade unions be in the development of learning strategies and the identification and planning of learning needs?'.

These questions I would argue are central to the success or otherwise of the EIS' LRs initiative, as at school level, the LRs will be (or should be) seen as conduits between the teachers and school management; school management will want to input into the CPD of its teachers and presently LRs do not have statutory bargaining rights. However, through the very nature of their work will be advising at an individual level on teachers' learning needs and strategies.

Alexandrou et al. (2005: 9) evaluating the Public and Commercial Services' Union's (PCS) ULRs scheme set out their stall by arguing that:

'...in the context of the British trade union movement's historic and continuing commitment to education...the energy, commitment, honesty and hopefulness of the ULR stands in stark contrast to the debacle of individual learning accounts'.

Whilst, Wallis et al. (2005: 283-284) take the view that:

'After almost two decades of government hostility and antipathy this [the ULR initiative] represents a significant gain for the British trade union movement, since the advancement of the learning agenda has been intimately connected to the issue of trade union revitalization'.

It is interesting to note the two different stances, one based on the educational and learning aspects and the other directed at the position of trade unions in contemporary Britain and their need to survive. This indicates that there are dual expectations of ULRs. Not only are they regarded as brokers or conduits of guidance and information with regard to learning and training in the workplace, they are also seen as trade union representatives. They are regarded as the new face of British unionism that can help to halt the decline in trade union membership by acting as ambassadors and recruiters for unions. A point highlighted by Wallis et al. (2005: 284) who state that:

> 'Not surprisingly, the expectations of ULRs amongst policy makers are high. ULRs, it is claimed, offer the potential of increased learning opportunities for individual members, new members for trade unions and improved performance for employers'.

This is backed up by Wood and Moore (2005: 24) who found that the:

> '...establishment of statutory rights to paid time-off for ULRs has clearly been a key development in the development of union learning'.

Whilst, Lee and Cassell (2004: 9) point out that the:

> '...UK government and an increasing number of employers have recognized the importance of promoting broad learning opportunities in the workplace. The statutory rights given to learning representatives in the UK will ensure that others will follow suit'

This is a key point in the literature in terms of workplace learning and training being inextricably bound up with trade unionism and will be examined further.

Trade Union Revitalisation Through Learning

Sutherland and Rainbird (2000:191) point out that the '... development of trade union strategy towards workplace learning is centrally concerned with questions of organisational renewal. Heery et al. (2004:3) argue that society expects them to change and evolve and that:

> '...the source of this pressure lies in deep-seated changes in the economy and society that are altering the structure of interests and preferences that workers are bringing to their employment and, by extension, to trade unions.

This, in turn, requires a new form of trade unionism better matched to the requirements of a changing workforce'.

Forrester (2001: 318-319) points out that developments such as ULRs are part of the trade unions modernising agenda that is aimed at giving them a new role and raison d'être following the reduction in their power and influence in the 1980s and 1990s. He backs this up by stating that if:

> 'Waddington (1995) is correct in suggesting that the 1980s and early years of the 1990s can be seen as a period in which British trade unions were "searching for an agenda", the role of workplace learning can be seen as being one of the agenda items in this search' (Forrester, 2001: 321).

Forrester (2005: 259) continues in this vein when he points out that:

> '...the promotion of lifelong learning by the new Labour government towards the end of the 1990s encouraged the TUC to be more expansive and confident of the possible contribution by trade unionists to this key policy objective'.

Stuart (2004:2) not only supports the sentiments of Forrester but argues that '...training and learning issues have attained a more strategic position in recent times'. He argues that:

> '...employees and employers may have different needs and interests in relation to learning and training, [and] much will depend on the employment relations in which ULRs operate, the nature of their engagement with employers and the trade union support structures into which they are inserted' (Stuart, 2004:1).

Dehmel (2005:47) enhances the debate by pointing out:

> '...the role of trade unions in encouraging participation [in learning] amongst employers and employees was strengthened, particularly through the introduction of the Union Learning Fund and new rights for Union Learning Representatives'.

The points made above are pertinent to the analysis of the EIS LRs as not only is the EIS taking a gamble with setting up such a group of lay representatives outside its "cultural norms" but the manner in which it is helping to deliver the *McCrone Agreement* will also impact on how its members perceive it is dealing with their CPD needs.

Heery et al. (2004:34) argue that:

> 'Unions' increasing engagement with workplace learning has stemmed from developments in training policy and the growing propensity of the state to use trade unions as agents of policy delivery in this area'.

This is a key point from the EIS perspective, as this is a journey into the unknown for the Institute and its LRs. Firstly how will the key stakeholders take to the LRs and secondly, will employers be sympathetic to another layer of representation that will seek time-off and other facilities which may well stretch the already tight finances of the Scottish education system?

Of further interest will be to examine from an EIS perspective whether the factor highlighted by Wood and Moore (2005: 28-30) who found that a significant number of formal learning agreements had been reached where there was an LR presence has occurred within Scottish education. Many of the ULRs felt that such an agreement was important in terms of securing for example, the long term future of a learning centre and that the main barrier to concluding more of these agreements were the employers. Significantly, they also found that learning was separate from the collective bargaining agenda but their case studies showed '...that union learning can have a positive outcome for both the unions and employers involved' with more than half their respondents stating that union learning encouraged greater cooperation with employers on learning issues (Wood and Moore, 2005: 31-34). This point then brings into question about how far cooperation and partnerships can be developed between unions and employers without it being seen to dilute what both stand for and strive for.

Partnership

Sutherland and Rainbird (2000:199-202) point out that '...some trade unions and many trade unionists believe that any form of partnership with management is a denial of the fundamental conflict of interest between workers and managers' but argue that learning partnerships should be distinguished from other workplace collective bargaining partnerships by highlighting the partnership approach behind the Ford EDAP, the *Return to Learn* partnership between Unison and employers and the Union Learning Fund that supports joint union/employer learning projects. However, they point out that if unions are to be successful they need to have an agenda in place that '...is independent of management'.

Munro and Rainbird (2000, 2004a) in their examination of the Unison/employer learning partnerships point out (based on previous work by Ackers and Payne, 1998) that such partnerships at national level are:

> '...seen as offering trade unions a way back into the mainstream of political and industrial life' (Munro and Rainbird, 2004a: 419).

They go on to argue that whilst there is no "blueprint" for such partnerships and the Unison approach is distinctive as it focuses specifically on workplace learning; the partnerships are often informal and are '...union-initiated, with a union-defined agenda, which has the membership benefits at its core' (Munro and Rainbird, 2004a: 420). They found clear benefits in such partnerships for trade union members and that they did not '...undermine workplace organisation and, in generating membership enthusiasm, have the potential (not always realised in practice) to enhance local union organisation. They also identified that the statutory rights for ULRs have '...implications for the significance of learning to union strategies and activities, as well as for the development of learning partnerships with employers' and their study showed that the '...partnership approach also allowed managers to consolidate and build on good working relationships with UNISON', particularly with branch secretaries based on mutual respect (Munro and Rainbird, 2004a: 421-427).

Based on their two case studies of healthcare trusts working with the unions Amicus and Unison to deliver lifelong learning opportunities to their employees, Haunch and Bennett (2002) develop this theme of partnership as being the underpinning of the success of the learning projects being evaluated. To a degree this is backed up by Forrester (2005: 261) based on his examination of other studies dealing with workplace learning where he points out:

> 'Despite the widespread debate surrounding union and employer partnerships...trade union workplace learning is increasingly undertaken, and encouraged, within an employer partnership relationship'.

This issue of partnership is significant as in the two previous chapters, the push for lifelong learning has been regarded as a partnership initiative amongst all stakeholders by this present administration; within the context of Scottish education and particularly the *McCrone Agreement* (SEED, 2001), partnership is a central tenet. However, the academic debate has not in the main dealt with this issue and has concentrated on the adversarial nature of learning in the workplace, particularly from a ULR perspective.

However, the optimism highlighted by the above debate must be tempered somewhat by the warnings of Terry (2003) picked up by Forrester (2005: 261-262) who points out that there is a:

> '...real danger...of partnerships possibly being a form of corporate-level "political" exchange, whereby unions forgo significant opportunities for challenging managerial

decisions in exchange for recognition of their procedural and institutional standing'.

As has been highlighted above trade union activity in workplace learning has increased significantly, with Forrester (2005: 258) arguing that '...the promotion of learning opportunities for members has emerged as an important success story' and goes on to point out that there has been a:

> '...political repositioning of trade unions and the TUC in particular, as important players in the government's lifelong learning policy agenda and institutional arrangements'.

Union Learning Representatives

The aim of this part of the book is to analyse the debate surrounding ULRs and identify certain issues or findings that can lend themselves to creating a basis for opening up the discussion in this area and possibly stimulating a polemical debate. Significantly, the available literature concentrates on manual and lower grade employees rather than what can be termed "white collar" professional personnel and does not take cognisance of the teaching profession.

The few articles and papers published in this field have in the main an industrial relations bent rather than one focussed on the ULRs themselves and their impact on workplace learning and employee professional development. They centre on the role of trade unions within the employer-employee relationship based on what can be regarded as the conflictual nature of such a relationship.

The Development of ULRs

Forrester (2001) and Payne (2001) were writing before LRs received statutory recognition and their following observations of LRs must firstly be regarded in a historical context and secondly they have been overtaken by events such as legislation. Forrester (2001: 321) rightly points out that:

'Although at a very early stage of development, learning representatives, it can be argued, are illustrative of the innovative learning openings currently being developed by unions'.

Whilst Payne (2001: 360) highlighted that some commentators have likened LRs to Health and Safety representatives but without the safety net of legislation This observation is clearly redundant in the face of legislative change as noted in the opening chapter as is Payne's (2001: 360) examples based on his previous work (Payne, 1999, 2000) and that of Ross (2000) who evaluated LRs in their formative stage of development being refused time-off by their employers and having to deal with the reluctance of educational providers to work in partnership with them.

In addition to these difficulties Forrester (2001: 323) highlighted that there was:

'...little existing regional organisation and expertise in unions generally, or within the TUC that can address the needs of local learning representatives' and that it is '...unlikely that the unions have the capacity or resources to initiate and sustain the development of workplace learning representatives'.

In relation to time-off, employers are not allowed to deny this to the representatives under the new legislation. However, this is not to say that this is a moot point as a LR can only be as effective as the support that he/she receives not only from their union but also from the employer and the next two chapters will examine whether the EIS LRs' employers are working to the spirit of the legislation as well as the letter of it. Hoque and Bacon (2006: 6-7) point out that the:

'...purpose of providing statutory provisions for ULRs was to increase the incidence of workplace training by supporting their role as independent trusted and well trained advisors for employees and as "allies" for managers in promoting learning'.

They go to argue that:

> '...it is important to take specific account of the possibility that the effectiveness of ULRs may be restricted by employer unwillingness to negotiate and consult on workplace training issues...especially if ULRs seek to promote a training agenda separate from employer requirements' (Hoque and Bacon, 2006: 7).

The issue of their relationship with educational providers was of interest as it has a bearing on not only their effectiveness but also their ability to service the needs of their colleagues and to become part of the structure of lifelong learning for teachers in Scotland. These are key points as Stuart (2004:3) picking up on arguments made by Munro and Rainbird (2004a) points out that the:

> '...broader regulatory frameworks governing health and safety are absent with regard to ULRs...and it is notable that the statutory provisions granted to ULRs do not extend to consultation and bargaining rights with regard to learning'.

Payne (2001: 336-367) points out that a central role of LRs is '...to gain vital support from employers for workplace learning programmes'. It seems from this argument that LRs can and should be regarded as a type of "bridge" between the trade unions and their members and employers in terms of brokering and facilitating workplace learning and development. In turn, this places a significant emphasis on the roles, responsibilities and abilities of LRs in terms of executing their function. This point is backed up by Forrester (2001: 322) who states that the:

> '...emergence of workplace learning representatives is an important stage in the development of union learning objectives. The vision of a nation-wide (or sector or company-wide) network of well trained and supported union learning representatives in regular contact with their local learning and training resources and agencies is a persuasive one',

and by the findings of Stuart and Robinson (2007: 4) in their analysis of training, union recognition and collective bargaining data from the 2004 Workplace Employment Relations Survey, in which they highlight that there are higher levels of consultation and negotiation in relation to training issues in workplaces that accept and recognise ULRs.

Indeed, it mirrors the activities and aspirations of the EIS and is a point that is being tested in this study. Calveley et al. (2003: 7) point out that:

> 'Initial evidence suggests that ULRs may act as signposts to a wide variety of education and training, including broad generic skills and specific skills, accredited and non-accredited courses, and provision that is directly job-related as well as that which is not'.

Basically, they are acting as "honest brokers" in relation to the current workplace learning agenda and this issue will be analysed further.

The ULR as a Learning Broker

Thursfield et al. (2004) briefly touch upon ULRs in their work that develops the concept of learning brokerage in the workplace. They argue it is an emerging phenomenon and that the policy of lifelong learning and getting more people to participate in learning contributes to '…this notion of the learning broker' (Thursfield et al., 2004: 371). This concept of a learning broker is key to understanding the trials and tribulations of the first set of EIS LRs, particularly in the light of Thursfield et al's. (2004: 372) following definition of what a learning broker is:

> 'The term learning broker suggests an agent whose role is to provide learners or employers with impartial advice of both a practical and pedagogical nature, and to unite learners, employers and training providers in a virtuous, mutually beneficial relationship'.

This definition encapsulates what a ULR should be and do and I concur with them that the whole issue of brokerage has not been problematised and is under-developed from both an academic and theoretical perspective, particularly from a ULR perspective. By using the underpinning concept of brokerage, it allows me in this book to develop and add to the academic and theoretical debate concerning ULRs, particularly from a Scottish teaching perspective.

Thursfield et al. (2004) regard ULRs as one type of learning broker (under the heading of Learning Adviser) and through their longitudinal study they have created an analytical framework based on the concepts of "power" and "autonomy". For them, power refers '...to the degree to which brokerage is embedded in a hierarchical relation to learners', whilst autonomy '...refers to the degree to which the broker is free from links with institutional management (Thursfield et al., 2004: 375). I would argue that this framework based on the above definitions fits in with the concept of ULRs, particularly the EIS LRs. It can be argued that since devolution and the *McCrone Report* (2000), the politics of education have changed as have the relationships between the key stakeholders with a new stakeholder on the scene in the form of teacher LRs. As such the concepts of power and autonomy described above impact on how the EIS LRs fulfil their roles and responsibilities.

These concepts are further underpinned by Thursfield et al. (2004: 376-385) describing the constraints on effective brokerage and the prerequisites for successful brokerage. They highlight three constraints, the first being organisational factors such as the relationship between and the competing interests of employers and employees as well as their respective workplace learning agendas. The second relates to '...the discourse surrounding the notion of learning' with the '...language used by the proponents of learning [becoming]...a barrier to learning and the third concerning '...the contradictions and tensions pertaining to the role of broker'. As for the prerequisites for successful brokerage they highlight what they term:

'...the significance of social cohesion and a sense of

ownership...Furthermore, effective brokerage is only likely to be seen in an environment where lifelong learning is not shackled by a narrow "workplace development agenda"'.

The Role and Characteristics of a ULR

Thursfield et al. (2004: 376-377) identify the key characteristics of a Learning Adviser (such as a ULR) and I believe the following characteristics help to conceptualise and theorise the roles and responsibilities of EIS LRs further. The key characteristics are:

- Command respect from fellow employees, prospective learners and managers
- Has no formal position within the organisation's hierarchy
- Has some form of power as they have emerged from the employee ranks, thus power '...emanates from the personal attributes of the broker'
- Has an ambassadorial role as they come from a similar background to those they are advising (McGiveny, 1999)
- Is autonomous from management structures

Significantly, they state that although employed by an organisation they are free to give what advice is '...deemed suitable' for the prospective learner and that they are '...acting in the interests of both the individual learner and the organisation'. This statement has resonance with the EIS LRs as basically this is their *raison d'être*. They go on to point out that the '...activities of the learning broker do not evolve independently of existing workplace relations' (Thursfield et al., 2004: 379). This is a pertinent point in relation to the EIS LRs as it can be safely said that they were borne out of the *McCrone Report* (2000).

The Chartered Institute of Personnel and Development (CIPD) (2004:2) states that the role of LRs in the workplace:

> '...provides a significant new source of expertise and engagement in promoting the learning agenda at work.

> As trusted members of the trade union, who are trained in their new roles, union learning representatives are well placed to provide support, encouragement and guidance to their members'.

Whilst the LRD (2005: 10) has produced a guide for teacher ULRs on behalf of the main teaching unions in England and Wales and in terms of the role of teacher LRs it states it could include the following:

- Equality of access for part-time, agency and supply teachers and those returning from maternity leave
- Developing mentoring schemes
- Identifying appropriate learning opportunities
- Promoting a whole-school approach to lifelong learning
- Promoting good work/life balance
- Being involved in helping to shape INSET days.

Significantly, it goes on to advise that the:

> '...role of the teacher ULR is not to assume or replicate the duties of either the local authority or the school CPD co-ordinator. Indeed, the teacher ULR role can complement those of the CPD co-ordinators' (LRD, 2005: 10).

Wallis et al. (2005: 287) based on the thoughts and ideas of Forrester (2001), Rainbird et al. (2003) and Munro and Rainbird (2004a) warn that LRs face '... a significant challenge' in terms of how they position themselves and how they are positioned by others. For example, they point out that the Government sees them supporting employers learning and training initiatives and that they may in turn be furthering the '...business needs' of organisations. Thus they state:

> 'A key issue for consideration, then, is how ULRs will be able to resolve the different needs of employers and employees, and promote opportunities that are of prime benefit to employees'.

This is a key issue for the EIS to consider in relation to the *raison d'être* for its LRs initiative, particularly as it is signed up to the McCrone recommendations in relation to CPD as outlined in the previous chapter and as Wallis et al. (2005: 287) point out '...much will depend here on the ability of trade unions to retain an independent agenda with respect to learning'. This is a crucial point for the EIS and its LRs as on the one hand they are by their own admission stakeholders and partners in the Scottish education sector but the Institute is also the single most powerful teacher representative body in Scotland that has not only to take cognisance of its members' views but also bargain on their behalf, including, on the issue of CPD. However, it has signed up to McCrone and are the EIS LRs merely acting on behalf of the Scottish Executive and local authorities in delivering the McCrone CPD initiative or are they acting in the best interests of their colleagues? This is a dilemma that will be examined in the forthcoming chapters.

Wallis et al. (2005: 287) point out that whilst LRs may well be successful in helping their colleagues; developing and advancing a learning agenda and '...generate new forms of union activism [and] union activists' it could bring them into conflict with the established order within their unions and create tensions between themselves and other trade union officials and representatives, who may have a set opinion as to what their role and activities should consist of. Thompson et al. (2007: 20) take this one step further in their evaluation of workplace learning initiatives in Scotland when they argue that as:

> '...a new representational role, and one that is still developing, there is a potential for ULRs to be isolated from other union activities and activists. Assimilating ULRs and their role into wider union structures is crucial'.

As highlighted above, this is a critical issue for the EIS, as it has been around a long time as have its traditions, structures and modus operandi, whilst the LR initiative is in its infancy and with at present no official provision made for "slotting in" the LRs into national and local structures. Thus, the relationship between LRs and their local associations may well prove critical not only to the acceptance of the LRs by the wider membership but also their success or otherwise. This point is further strengthened by Stuart's (2004:6) concerns that questions still remain as to '...how ULRs are being inserted in the traditional structures and activities of trade unions'.

Moore and Wood (2007: 11) help to take the debate of the role of ULRs further with their findings that ULRs should play a far greater role in recruitment. If this is the case then it may well help not only integrate learning representatives into union structures but be accepted by both lay and full-time officials. As Moore and Wood (2007: 11) state:

> 'Overwhelmingly, union learning officers agree that ULRs should and do play a role in recruitment. In one large union it is the union's policy (recognised in recent conference policy and communicated through the union's ULR handbook and guide for full-time officers), that all learning activities should have an organising outcome'.

ULRs as New Activists

Haunch and Bennett (2002: 11-13) point out that the push for lifelong learning has created new activists in terms of ULRs who had not held a union position before and volunteered because of their positive learning experiences. Interestingly, they highlight that this new cadre of activist as they term them have embraced their position because they '...like the learning side of it, not any of the union side'. This development in turn has positively impacted on participation in union affairs and membership numbers. Significantly, there was clear evidence that the unions were able to show the two trusts that '...promoting learning was a shared agenda, in that its outcomes were of benefit to both sides of the industrial divide' (Haunch and Bennett, 2002:11).

Forrester (2001: 323-324) backs up the points made above when he highlights that enthusiasm for learning was a key motivator for many volunteering to become LRs but goes on to warn that important as it is, it is '...likely to be insufficient in navigating the contested and unhelpful environment of many workplaces'. Stuart (2004:6) states that he has found examples of '...outright employer hostility to engaging with ULRs' and that '...employers [are] attempting to "incorporate" them within management functions'. In addition to these factors, Shelley (2006: 5) in his study of the Hertfordshire Trade Union Learning Centre found some evidence that a few ULRs after they had been trained where not active once they returned to their workplaces. These observations are a clear warning to all unions, including the EIS and will be returned to in the following chapters.

This warning can in part be tempered by the further positive findings of Haunch and Bennett (2002:13) who point out that the ULRs in their study have extended their role by:

> '...going out to job fairs and schools and promoting learning and the NHS as a career, attending induction days and mentoring staff through appraisals, IT and vocational training'

Significantly, there was also evidence of negotiation in terms of them helping colleagues to identify learning opportunities and negotiating on their behalf with management to get them to access the learning they required. This is a key point as by the nature of their stated role both within the legislation and in the unions they represent, ULRs are not seen as having a negotiating role but as the role develops, so will the negotiating aspect of it. Haunch and Bennett (2002:13) argue '...all union positions are to a degree about negotiation and bargaining on behalf of your members'.

However, this argument is in part tempered by the observations of Hoque and Bacon (2006: 7-8) in their analysis of training incidence in the UK linked to trade union recognition and ULRs, who point out that the *Employment Act 2002* (Parliament, 2002):

> '...does not provide bargaining rights over training...It

is possible therefore that ULRs do not increase training provision because employers expect them to support existing training strategies that match provision to business need rather than identify any significant step-change in approach. Additionally, unions may have deliberately located ULRs in workplaces where managers do not negotiate or consult unions over training in the hope that their presence would encourage the development of training activity in these workplaces'.

This is supported by Stuart (2004:5) who has examined evidence from the TUC and other sources and highlights that '…ULRs are establishing a dialogue with employers around the learning agenda' and that they are "negotiating" with employers as well as reaching formal and informal agreements as to their roles and responsibilities within the workplace, which interestingly include sitting on training committees and being involved in developing training policies. He goes on to argue that the evidence to date suggests:

> '…a significant network of enthusiastic ULRs are now active in British workplaces and they are having an impact, in terms of encouraging individuals to take up learning and developing formal union-management relations around learning' (Stuart, 2004:6).

Of particular significance is Haunch and Bennett (2002:14) observing the added benefits that one of the trusts was gaining from the activities of the ULRs by pointing out that a:

> '…network of over twenty learning representatives provide outreach work for the HR department not just in terms of training needs analysis and learner support but also in retention and recruitment'.

This brings into question whether these particular ULRs are merely an adjunct of their HR department or their role has developed to such a degree that they are truly working in partnership with their organisation to not only help with the learning needs of their fellow employees but to also improve the efficiency and effectiveness of the Trust. Particularly, as Haunch and Bennett (2002: 14) highlight that some of the ULRs have either been promoted to work in their Trust's training department or been seconded to work on specific projects. Wallis and Stuart (2007: 17) in their analysis of workplace learning agreements take this debate one step further when they point out and argue that within their case study organisations the:

> '...development of ULR capacity has also enlarged the internal pool of labour available to the human resources/ training departments...While such individuals may, of course, be lost to the union movement, paradoxically it may be the case that they are better placed to advance union concerns in relation to the learning agenda within their new roles.'

Calveley et al. (2003: 17) raise the issue of the profile of the ULRs based on TUC statistics and they showed that of the LRs that had been trained as of 2002, ten per cent had not held a representative position before and they tended to be women and younger members. This seems to go against the stereotypical view most people have of union representatives being older white males doing deals in smoke-filled rooms. This leads Calveley et al. (2003: 17) to argue that LRs are:

> '...seen as a mechanism for promoting equality of opportunity in the workplace, partnership between employers and trade unions and possible union renewal. The interesting aspect of this argument is that learning and development are notable by their absence'.

The Independence of ULRs

Calveley et al. (2003:19) using union literature as a basis argue that a ULR should be an independent and trusted representative whose role should be to improve the employability and skills of employees which in turn will enable them to be equipped to adapt to change more easily and '...increase participation in workplace training'.

This type of activity rightly brings into question the independence of the ULRs and Haunch and Bennett (2002:14) defend them in their study by arguing that ULRs have not '...become merely "incorporated" within HR. Rather it demonstrates the shared asset that the learning representatives have become for both the Trust and its unions'.

However, as Munro and Rainbird (2004b:155) argue:

> '...it is important to make the distinction between training for employee need and training for employer or business need. Training for business need primarily benefits the organisation and there may be few or only indirect benefits to the employee...In contrast, training for employee need contributes' to workers' broader development and employability and does not restrict training to the needs of the current job'.

In relation to the EIS LRs, one of the issues that was explored in this study was whether they have been able to pursue a CPD agenda that benefits their colleagues or have been "railroaded" into following the developmental plans of local authorities and schools.

The Impact of ULRs in the Workplace

Since the inception of ULRs there have been relatively few evaluations of how they have progressed and impacted upon their organisations, colleagues and their unions. This is significant as there are now over 18,000 trained ULRs (Clough, 2007: 19) who Alan Johnson (then Secretary of State for Education and Skills) points out helped over 150,000 people to access learning in 2006 and that the '...nation now has an army of union learning representatives', who along with New Labour's *Learning Agenda* are one of the great success stories of the past decade (Johnson, 2007: 1-5).

To date I have identified fifteen significant evaluations and surveys that have examined ULRs in any detail. These have been undertaken by Cowen et al. (2000) for the TUC; Ross (2000 and 2001) for the MSF union (now Unison) the LRD (2003, 2006) for the TUC , Cutter (2003) for the Southern and Eastern Region TUC, TUC (2003), Alexandrou et al. (2005) for the PCS, Wood and Moore (2005) for the ULF, Stuart et al. (2003) and Wallis et al. (2005) for the Yorkshire and Humberside TUC, Cassell and Lee (2005a, 2005b), Hoque and Bacon (2006) and Donnelly and Kiely (2007) for the South West Region of the TUC.

All these studies can be regarded as a concise overview of developments to date. My examination of the results of these evaluations, show that they have all broadly raised the same issues and produced similar findings. Taking these factors into consideration, I aim to use the Cowen et al. report (2000) as the basis, as it is the first detailed study to date that covers a large number of learning representatives from a significant number of trade unions. It must be noted that this study was carried out before ULRs were granted statutory rights, so there cannot be a like for like comparison and where the results from the other evaluations deviate significantly (particularly those undertaken after statutory recognition was introduced) from this study they will be highlighted and discussed.

In their study, Cowen et al. (2000) addressed the following four key questions (which have resonance for this analysis):

- *Who becomes a learning representative?*
- *What success have they achieved?*
- *What kind of support is given to learning representatives by unions and others?*
- *What barriers do learning representatives face in achieving their workforce learning objectives?*

In relation to the demographic details of ULRs, the researchers found that 62.1% were male, 37.9% were female; less than 2% were from ethnic minority groups; 45% were aged 45-59 (Cowen et al., 2000: 8-9). Whilst, Wood and Moore (2005; 10-11) found that 77% were male; 23% female and 5% from ethnic minorities and significantly, 68% being long standing union members with an average membership of nineteen years.

Interestingly, the study found that 91% of ULRs were active as union members in other ways such as being a shop steward, organiser or health and safety representative. The remaining 9% are new and are more likely to be female (Cowen et al., 2000: 10-11). Cutter (2003:10), Wood and Moore (2005:11), Wallis et al. (2005: 296-297) and LRD (2006: 2) found that 21%, 22%, 27% and 36% respectively were new activists. This is a key factor as in less than five years the number of new activists has more than trebled if not quadrupled and in this period LRs received statutory recognition. This may well have a bearing on non-activists taking up the mantle of learning in the workplace. Interestingly, the LRD (2006) notes that the new activists are more likely to be women in over 50% of cases and one-in-five will invariably be younger as they will be 36 years old or under.

Significantly, Wood and Moore (2005: 11-13) point out that the new activists described themselves as '...active on learning but not involved in other aspects of the union' and that the significant majority of new activists (76%) did not join their union because they believed in trade unionism. More than half of them volunteered to become a LR because of their commitment '...to education within the context of union activity' based on their own positive experiences of learning.

This backed up by the findings of Cassell and Lee (2005a) and Donnelly and Kiely (2007: 4) and the latter found that ULRs come:

> '...to learning activism for the first time through one of two routes. First, there are those that are converted to the learning cause through experiencing union-led workplace learning itself and are mentored into the role. Second, others develop an interest in the union learning agenda and either volunteer themselves or are talent-spotted and recruited subsequently'.

Whilst Wallis et al. (2005: 297) highlight the alternative

view espoused by Smith (2003) in relation to new activists that many of them are:

> '...often motivated to become ULRs by instrumental considerations; regarding the ULR position primarily as a conduit to a stronger curriculum vitae or training opportunities, while lacking a strong attachment to trade union principles and goals'.

This view has only been promulgated by Smith but it is worth noting and was pursued in the survey of EIS LRs.

In relation to their training, 92.5% of the ULRs were satisfied with the training they received for their new role, whilst 93.3% stated that to some degree they were utilising the skills acquired in the training to some degree (Cowen et al., 2000: 12-13).

Interestingly, Cutter (2003:11) found that:

> 'Learning representatives that are union activists can have the benefits of: more developed negotiating skills; strong links into other union structures; and recognition from the employer as an individual that knows their needs of their colleagues'.

This factor will undoubtedly have a bearing on the success or otherwise of the EIS LRs but as Cutter (2003:11) goes on to point out there could well be disadvantages to having more than one union role as: '...Time and resource constraints can reduce the availability of the rep to develop and support learning provision' and some of the stakeholders interviewed argued that it would be preferable to have new activists in the role as they would have a genuine interest in the "learning agenda" but also recognised that they would require guidance and support.

In terms of how they used their time and the activities they were involved in, the representatives highlighted that 90% of them spent 5 or less hours per week on ULR duties; 71% promoted the value of learning to colleagues and 79% offered learning advice and guidance. Significantly, 50% of the ULRs were involved in negotiating learning issues with their employer and just under a half were involved in trying to access funding for learning (Cowen et al., 2000: 14-16).

The research revealed that 37.9% of the representatives offered support only to colleagues from the same union; just 12.4% offered support to any union member on their site and significantly 46.4% offered support to any employee within their workplace (Cowen et al., 2000: 16). Wallis et al. (2005: 289) have also noted the significance of non-members asking for advice and guidance and highlighted the debate that ULRs are not just about the learning agenda but are inextricably linked to the organising agenda and went on to show from their survey results that:

> '...half the non-union members that approached ULRs for advice and guidance subsequently joined, or made enquiries about joining a trade union'.

The learning representatives were asked to identify the type of support they received from their union and the following in descending order of importance were highlighted:

- Training and guidance (71%).
- Information on new learning initiatives (58%).
- Support from officers (54%).
- Networking opportunities (28%).
- Information on the activities of other ULRs (23%) (Cowen et al., 2000: 18).

However, Wood and Moore (2005: 15-19) found support from full-time and senior lay officials to be variable with a number being reluctant to get involved with LRs because of their concerns surrounding LRs and the partnership role that was part of their remit. They also found that a fifth of their respondents had never attended a local branch meeting. Cassell and Lee (2005a: 27) also found this to be the case because '...the branch did not understand the role of the learning representative. These factors along with Wood and Moore (2005: 40-41) highlighting that very few unions in their survey '...formally recognise the ULR role in their rulebooks or constitutions' and that union learning is still not a mainstream issue for unions brings into question the integration of LRs into union structures and systems and their ability to be able to carry out their roles and responsibilities. This point was pursued during the analysis of the EIS LRs.

Cowen et al. (2000: 19-22) pre-statutory recognition found that 70% of the representatives got paid time-off for their ULR training, whilst 52.3% were given paid time-off to carry out some of their duties and less than one third received other support such as access to rooms and equipment. Significantly, 22.3% of the representatives were dissatisfied with the support they received and within this group the female ULRs were found to be more dissatisfied than their male counterparts. The representatives argued that they wanted:

- More support from senior management.
- More time for ULR duties.
- More access to learning resources.
- More learning resource space and equipment (Cowen et al., 2000: 19-22).

Wood and Moore (2005: 25) found that LRs are more likely to get time-off for training than for other ULR activities and a significant number undertook '...basic activities in their own time'. This is a key issue from an EIS perspective because if employers hinder the EIS LRs in this manner this will also have repercussions as to how effectively they can operate.

Wallis et al. (2005:290-291) reported that the majority of their LR cohort '...were not reliant upon management support for their activities' and go on to argue this could indicate a lack of support from their employers but '...it could also be suggestive of ULRs retaining their independence from management in relation to the learning agenda'. They also point out that a third of their respondents '...had attempted to negotiate with management over training issues, with the majority reporting positive outcomes arising from this activity'.

The study investigated the impact and achievements of the representatives and found that 80.2% felt that their work was having a positive impact on learning in their workplace and it included the following:

- Helping colleagues improve their basic skills.
- Improving the culture of learning at work.
- Helping colleagues with little or no experience of learning.
- Encouraging colleagues to continue learning.

31% also felt that their work was having other effects such as the positive impact on the culture of learning at work (Cowen et al., 2000: 23-24). Wood and Moore (2005: 21) found that a number of LRs had carried out workplace learning needs surveys that had a positive effect. Whilst, Wallis et al. (2005: 292-294) stated that a number of ULRs negotiated time-off for colleagues to undertake learning activities and sat on steering committees to:

> '...develop formal policies in relation to training and development'.

They also noted the interest amongst ULRs in developing a more strategic approach to their role where

> '...they would work more closely with management and have a major influence over training budgets, and the formulation of training and development policies'.

Alexandrou et al. (2005: 21-23) point out why LRs have had such a positive impact by highlighting that from an organisational perspective their LR cohort had been able to identify the most urgent demands for skills (which in this case was information technology) through interaction with members. They stated that '...their conversations with members were confidential and that they would not reveal their content to managers' and the LRs found that '...they were able to talk with their colleagues ...[and this]...aspect of being a trusted fellow worker who will keep what is said confidential is a major strength'. They go on to note that: 'Overwhelmingly, the success of the role will depend on the enthusiasm and willingness of the representatives', which they found in abundance when they interviewed the LRs.

Significantly, 19.2% of the ULRs felt that they were not making an impact (Cowen et al., 2000: 23-24) and Wallis et al. (2005: 296) may have part of the answer for this in their study when they state that:

> '...some ULRs have not sought to negotiate with their employers because they lacked the necessary skills and experience, whilst others who are already bargaining with employers, even on an informal basis, may need to develop additional skills in order to maximise their effectiveness'.

In part it may also have something to do with the learning representatives' relationship with their branch as Donnelly and Kiely (2007: 5) have found that the ULRs involved in their evaluation:

> '...recognise a continuum between learning activism at one extreme and branch activism at the other, nonetheless they differ as to where they choose to locate themselves on such a spectrum, when invited to do so...a polarisation emerges based on background such that those new to activism tend to define themselves more narrowly by reference to learning than other "mainstream" union issues compared to those taking on learning representation in addition to their other branch roles. Some new "learning activists" even report themselves as rarely attending formal branch forums or partaking in broader branch activities'

The representatives were asked how their achievements were being monitored. 60% stated that they personally maintained records, whilst 75% could give an estimate of outcomes achieved, which included the following:

- Promoting the benefits of learning.
- Giving advice and guidance on learning.
- Undertaking learning needs assessments.
- Helping to access funding for learning.
- Helping colleagues attend courses.
- Helping colleagues to open up ILAs
  (Cowen et al., 2000: 25-26).

Interestingly, the survey found that the representatives identified certain barriers with regard to their position. 78.6% stated that they faced some form of difficulty in carrying out their role. The key barriers they identified are:

- Lack of time for ULR activities.
- Lack of interest or even suspicion from colleagues.
- Lack of support from management.
- Problems in finding suitable courses to suit (shift) workers' needs.
- Limited availability of ILAs, where these had been promoted as a method of supporting learners into learning.
- Lack of formal recognition within the union structure (Cowen et al., 2000: 28-29).

Cutter (2003: 29-41) found that 10% of her respondents had been inactive since completing their training and in the main this was due to the lack of support from their employer but other factors that contributed to this inactivity included lack of support from their branch; constraints on their time and finding it difficult to pursue activities in small organisations. These factors linked with problems getting paid time-off coupled with '…an employer's lack of understanding of the learning representative role and little structured support from the union' meant that LRs were more likely to report that they were not achieving anything positive. Alexandrou et al. (2005: 23-24) support these findings, particularly highlighting the lack of understanding managers have of LRs with this following statement: '…He thinks my role is to tell him what people need and then tell them to do it. He doesn't understand that I'm not management and what I do is different'. This coupled with managers only paying lip-service to CPD and being afraid to give employees learning opportunities in case they lost them are issues that could well have a bearing as to how the EIS LRs navigate themselves through schools.

The researchers asked the ULRs how the barriers to learning amongst their work colleagues could be lifted and to state the key factors that they considered would be most effective in motivating more colleagues to take part in learning activities. The representatives identified a number of factors but the four main ones were:

- Paid time-off for learning.
- Funding to spend on learning.
- Access to learning resources during work hours.
- Encouragement from senior management (Cowen et al., 2000: 29-30).

Cutter (2003: 49-57) adds that LRs want more time-off to carry out their duties, and additional training and '...expert advice from their union/TUC'. She goes on to recommend that LRs keep a "learner log" to be used '...as a tool to identify learning reps' needs'.

Teacher Trade Union Activity

The discussion above has concentrated quite rightly on workplace learning and the impact of ULRs. However, there is a need to understand how a teacher trade union and its representatives operate within a school environment. The aim is to briefly highlight the debate from both a North American and British perspective concentrating on how teacher unions behave and deal with professional development. This approach is being taken to further inform the debate as well as the research findings based on the primary research. It is important to note Stevenson's (2003: 343) finding when reviewing the literature in this field (which is comparatively sparse compared to other sectors) that '...they had little to say about the role of [teaching] unions in the workplace. Ironside and Seifert (1995) have tackled the issue of industrial relations in schools but this work was published well over a decade ago and is now regarded as a historical document due to the pace of change in the education sector and I have concentrated on recent writings that are of more direct relevance to the issues being examined in this book.

Teacher Trade Unions and Professional Development

Healy (1999: 212) in her study of the National Union of Teachers (NUT) and teacher career development points out that unions have always been involved in this area:

> '...particularly in relation to the perceived equity associated with both the allocation of career development resources such as training and with decisions surrounding career progression'.

This is clearly in line with the current activities of the EIS in relation to LRs and CPD and as Bascia (2000: 386) points out that North American trade unions are now '...focussing increased attention on their membership' and this is primarily directed at their professional development which she argues is '...not uniformly popular with their members'.

Kerchner (2001: 220) adds substance to this point when he states that teacher unions in the USA '...have broken the bounds of industrial unionism and have created a tentative stake in organizing as mental workers rather than industrial workers'. Whilst Poole (2000: 107-110) argues that teachers can only improve through professional development and "renewal" and this can in part be achieved by a positive input from teachers' unions. Participants in her study stated that '...the union should pursue ...PD [professional development] interests as well as education quality'. This is clearly the case in Scotland with the *McCrone Agreement* (SEED, 2001) and the EIS' involvement in the CPD process through its LRs initiative.

These observations have a resonance with the EIS activities centred around CPD and the LRs initiative based on its heavy involvement with the *McCrone Agreement* (SEED, 2001). Particularly, as Bascia (2000:387) points out that in Canada and the USA:

> '...many teachers unions' professional development strategies focus on helping their members to respond to educational policy demands, especially when policy makers do not accompany such mandates with technical

assistance or clear examples of what changes in practice might look like'.

This is important from a British perspective as Healy (1999: 221) highlights that '...educational reform on head teachers has enhanced their power as a result of devolved budgeting' and this is a factor that will come into play with the EIS and was examined in relation to the primary research.

As Healy (1999: 226) found, teachers '...recognised the crucial relationship that exists between state action, teaching as a profession and teachers' own careers', which encapsulates the *McCrone Agreement* and the EIS' response to it in a nutshell. Whilst Bascia (2000: 399) points out that in some teacher unions in the USA, '...professional development priorities influence collective bargaining', for example, funding and time-off to study have found themselves negotiated into agreements.

Teacher Union Activity

Stevenson (2003: 341) points out that in British teaching the '...tradition of collective organisation is as old as state education, and today teachers represent one of the most highly unionised sectors of any occupational grouping' and has in fact started to increase membership in recent years unlike most other sectors of the economy. In turn he goes on to state that this should be of considerable interest, particularly as '...the environment within they function has clearly changed' (Stevenson, 2003: 342).

Bascia (2000: 397) succinctly sums up teacher trade unionism as follows in terms of what drives teachers to become representatives. She states they are '...teachers who recognize potential opportunities in union involvement that are not obvious to the majority of their colleagues'. Whilst the flipside to this definition is the one put forward by Stevenson (2003: 348) in his discussion on "active workplace representation" when he points out that there is a need for further clarification because there is a need to recognise '...that it is perfectly possible for a school representative to play an active role in promoting the union to its members, but they take no part in representing their individual and collective interests to management' and this may well be the case with the EIS LRs who by the nature of their role do not have official or statutory bargaining powers. This is compounded by Stevenson's (2003: 350) finding that that although school union representatives had contact with head teachers over a wide range of issues but overall '...contact is clearly limited to a relatively few instances'.

Stevenson (2003: 355) points out that due to the recent devolvement of responsibility to school management level the teaching unions will have '...to consider how they most effectively support their school-based representatives' in terms of providing them with suitable information and training and how best to deploy their full-time and lay officials. He argues because of this significant shift it:

> '...is important, therefore to develop a better understanding of the role that school union representatives play in shaping the interplay between teachers and their managers in school' Stevenson (2005: 220).

This is clearly one of the key issues being addressed in this study from a LR perspective but it will be interesting to examine Stevenson's (2005: 220) assertion that in this changed environment:

> '...the role of the school representative can be crucial not only in shaping key issues affecting teachers' experience of work, but also in developing the future capacity of the union organisation'.

This backs up Carter's (2004: 137-138) observation that in the UK teaching unions such as the NUT are having to deal with the issue of union renewal due to the "radical restructuring" of the public sector in the 1980s. This can be directly linked to the EIS and its LRs initiative as it is an example of a teaching union getting to grips with the modern day realities of what Carter (2004: 141) points out is an education sector that '...has been the object of numerous reforms and other initiatives'. However,

Stevenson (2005: 221-222) highlights a significant observation by Ozga (1987) in her study of the NUT in which she argues that:

> '...within schools many union representatives took on a significant role for the union but they often explicitly rejected becoming involved in the "union machine", which was perceived as bureaucratic, procedural and patriarchal'.

This is a factor that will be explored in the following chapters as the EIS is a long-established traditional representative body that has its own historical way of doing things and traditional structures and systems in place but has now veered from its comfort zone with the radical (from its perspective) introduction of LRs. How they are accepted and assimilated into the union at all levels will be a mark of how successful this initiative will be. This is a pertinent point because as Clough (2005: 16) points out:

> 'Most unions do not have any formal policies in place that are designed to integrate ULRs into union structures'.

Calveley and Healy (2003: 97-99) on the backdrop of what they term '...radical education reform in England and Wales' warn that greater decentralisation '...has created a managerial role for head teachers, with responsibility for financial and human resources devolved to local school managers from the local education authority (LEA)' and that '...local union structures may be too fragile to withstand managerial and competitive pressures'. This is a key point as the same applies to Scotland and as the LRs can be described as fledgling union representatives, they may not be at all effective if head teachers either regard them as a threat or as part of the adversarial bargaining forum that naturally exists. This issue was examined because of its importance and significance to the success or otherwise of the EIS' LRs initiative.

However, it is important to note that the LRD (2005: 9) has

identified a number of benefits that school management may accrue in working with teacher LRs. They are:

- Building positive relationships with head teachers and employers of teachers
- Providing the opportunity to address inequalities in access to learning and training opportunities
- Assisting head teachers to meet the requirements of the contractual right to a reasonable work/life balance which teachers now have by providing information about non-work related opportunities
- Helping to shape INSET days to meet teachers' needs
- Improving retention and morale
- Making potential financial savings
- Providing learning opportunities for teachers to change or develop their role.

Stevenson (2005: 229-232) highlights that there is a need to have some type of formality '...where representatives are involved in a recognised and agreed process'. This will obviously give them greater legitimacy with the management as '...it is increasingly likely that new issues will draw school representatives into more negotiating and possibly greater formality'. He takes this one step further when surmising that:

> '...as new forms of representation emerge, often based around new workplace issues...school representatives will require micro-political skills in order to maximise their effectiveness'.

This last statement encapsulates the situation that the EIS LRs now find themselves in and as Stevenson (2005: 232) points out teaching unions must '...consider how they support and develop the role of their school representative...[and]...must give consideration to how they try to connect the formal and informal elements of union organisation and activity'. These issues were examined in the case of the EIS LRs as they are key to how they are accepted by their colleagues and other stakeholders.

Kerchner (2001: 223) adds to this by bringing in the issue of partnership between teacher unions and other stakeholders by pointing out that in the USA they '...have participated in efforts to create national standards through membership in the New Standards Project [and] the National Commission on Teaching'. This is akin to the EIS and its involvement with *McCrone* and further substantiated by Poole (2000: 105) who states that '...Ec [economic] welfare and PD have a process connection – both can be negotiated and become part of collective agreements'.

It can be argued that the setting up of the LRs initiative is a move in this direction and one that sets the EIS aside from the vast majority of teaching unions not only in the UK but the world. Bascia (2000: 396) clearly demonstrates this is the case when she argues that if:

> 'Teachers unions that are serious about professional development of their members need to recognize how their own actions contribute, through the many dimensions of the work they do as organizations, to the narrowing or expansion of teachers' authority and capacity to act'.

Additionally, Bascia (2000: 399-400) goes on to argue that if teacher unions are serious about professional development and getting their representatives to be active and effective in this area, they in turn must have the structures in place; ensure meetings are relevant and accessible and be able to disseminate the right information.

These are crucial points if the EIS LRs are to flourish and imbed themselves and as has been highlighted above there is a need not only to recognise these representatives as legitimate union representatives but also to give them all the support they require and embed them in the union's culture, structures and constitution. In turn this will make them bona-fide representatives in the eyes of their colleagues and the school and local authority management they have to deal with. If this occurs then it will negate the point put forward by Kerchner (2001: 227) that embracing '...the educational quality agenda represents a generational change that has not yet played out as either belief or organizational reality'. As Kerchner astutely observes:

> 'Teaching, like other service sector jobs, can be "dumbed down" or "smartened up". The question of direction may be the most crucial labor battle of the next decade'.

However, it is important to note the thoughts of Stevenson (2007: 242) when he talks about *reform unionism*. He states that this description highlights a teacher union's '...willingness to bargain constructively for change in relation to government policy and teachers' conditions of service'. However, he does warn that teacher unions engaging in such '...social partnership have allied themselves with policies that can be deeply unpopular with teachers'. This may well be the case with the *21st Century Agreement,* in particular the CPD and Chartered Teacher elements of it and will be analysed in relation to the forthcoming chapters.

The following chapter begins to analyse the findings of the primary research and draws on Ball's (1993) policy trajectory and Bowe et al's (1992) context of practice. It highlights how the ULRs policy has been interpreted and implemented, concentrating on the views of key stakeholders; the demographic profile of LRs and the support and training they have received to date.

5

The Place and Position of Learning Representatives

Introduction

This chapter deals with how the EIS LRs are viewed by other stakeholders in the Scottish education system and will then go on to highlight the demographic profile of the first cohort; why they chose to become LRs; their thoughts on their training and how the Institute looks after them.

The View of Education Stakeholders

The GTCS does not have an official policy on LRs but Mathew MacIver (2006: 1-2), its Chief Executive has the following views on them:

'I have always seen the advent of Learning Representatives as an indication by the EIS that it has returned to its educational roots. The EIS has helped to shape educational policy in Scotland since its formation in 1847. Towards the end of the 20th Century it did tend to concentrate all its efforts on pay and conditions of service. Whilst doing that it did drift away from placing itself in the centre of informing educational policy.

As far as the EIS is concerned I believe that Learning Representatives are quite integral to a return of its educational roots.

Together with Learning Representatives I see the involvement of the EIS with the University of Paisley in terms of the Chartered Teacher Programme as part of that whole process.

I have always applauded that strategy by the EIS and I think that Learning Representatives should be seen within that general educational context.

I see Learning Representatives as an integral part of the whole CPD process in Scotland. It appeared to me that Learning Representatives indicate that the EIS is well aware that a new world of CPD is emerging and that the EIS must be at the centre of it.

I feel that Learning Representatives continue to operate at a level which is of critical importance to the practising teacher. They will know the needs of classroom teachers better than anyone. It is in that critical area then that Learning Representatives are crucial. They will have credibility in the classroom that others will not.

I applaud the idea that Learning Representatives should also inhabit the world of further education. I have always believed that we should not create a two strand system in Scotland. We have to develop a world where we are a family of professional educators and that is why the integration of further education into this whole Learning Representatives adventure is so important.

In conclusion, therefore, you will understand that my perspective is slightly different from the norm. I am very excited by them. I am very excited that the EIS is developing them and I hope they will become an important part of the fabric of Scottish education'.

These comments are backed up by Learning and Teaching Scotland (LTS) whose Chief Executive, Bernard McLeary (2005) states that '…We fully support them; we support them in principle and want to offer them practical support to develop their role'. He highlighted that the LTS has offered the EIS LRs workshops, information and updates on key curriculum and educational issues and that he had attended award ceremonies for LRs at the EIS' headquarters.

Interestingly, he pointed out that in his previous position as the Director of Education for Inverclyde Council, his approach towards LRs was to support the EIS bid for trade union funding for its LRs initiative and elaborated on this by stating that it was due to his '...support for the model of the extended professional'. He is looking for teachers to be the extended professional and will support any initiative that will achieve this. This is in no small part due to his belief in the idea of the reflective practitioner and does not see why a trade union should not be at the forefront of reflective practice which can be achieved through LRs. He went on to add that the LRs '...are an embodiment of the *McCrone Agreement*... [and]...that it is about the teaching profession of the 21st Century and the LRs are part of this' (McLeary, 2005).

Bernard McLeary (2005) stated that the LTS is looking for more consultation at local authority and school level and the LRs can be part of this consultation process. He went on to add that in terms of where the LRs fit in the Scottish education system they '...have a high potential to fit into the delivery of CPD and of the reflective practitioner and they fit into the new way of being a teacher'. He expanded upon this by stating that teachers need to start and continue to be reflective practitioners for their whole careers based on CPD and the LRs are a central element of '...the brokerage and mentoring potentiality' linked to this.

In terms of the LTS vision for the future for the LRs, Bernard McLeary (2005) stated that they fit into what the LTS wants in terms of communities of practice and that the LRs are a community of practice. It is also about being reflective practitioners and for him the modern role of a trade union, which goes beyond the protection of terms and conditions of employment.

Jim O'Brien (2005), Vice Dean of the University of Edinburgh's School of Education is equally positive of the LRs initiative which he personally welcomes and that he is:

> *'...pleased to see that we have moved away from industrial trade unionism and while I recognise there is a place for that and there will be times when strategies that might be termed historically as industrial will be required, it appears to be*

that the EIS is attempting to position itself at the forefront of the re-culturing exercise in Scottish education post-McCrone and involvement in professional development in my view is a key factor in this.

I believe that the EIS has positioned itself astutely in the Scottish context as a major partner of the Scottish Executive – Government, as a major player in this policy – the UK policy of learning representatives. It might be suggested that this is because this is the way the EIS and other trade unions will survive and flourish in the future and putting such a constant as this gives the EIS scheme another dimension. It is interesting to speculate on what the EIS strategy in relation to learning representatives is and how the EIS will keep the scheme going; how it keeps potential radical representatives in check and how it progresses and grows the number of learning representatives'.

Overall, the comments above indicate a positive response to the EIS' LRs initiative and that partnership is regarded as a key factor in the LRs being effective. Of equal significance is Mathew MacIver's (2006: 1-2) observation that the LRs have the credibility with those that matter the most, the teachers themselves. However, the key question is how is the initiative functioning in practice? In the remainder of this chapter I will begin to attempt to find some answers to this question based on the experiences of the first cohort of LRs and the observations of the stakeholders to some of the issues that the LRs raised.

Demographic Profile of the Learning Representatives

As stated above thirty one questionnaires were distributed and twenty nine were returned, which meant there was a 93.5% response rate. Of these respondents seventeen (54.8%) were women and twelve (38.7%) were men. These figures in part represent the gender balance of the EIS' total membership, where women are significantly in the majority. As of March

2005, the total membership of the EIS stood at 55,677, of which 42,014 (75.5%) were women and 13,663 (24.5%) were men (EIS, 2005). At this early stage it is worthy of note that proportionately more men than women volunteered to become LRs. In one sense this ties in with the findings of other LR evaluations most notably those of Cowen et al. (2000), Wood and Moore (2005) and LRD (2006). However, in terms of direct comparison with other unions, the EIS leads the way with more than twice as many female LRs as any other union.

It was noted at an early stage in the research process that the issue of gender could have a bearing on how LRs connect or otherwise with colleagues in terms of their representative role. However, no evidence came to light to suggest that the gender of a LR either adversely or positively affected their effectiveness or their relationships with colleagues, school management, CPD advisers or local authority personnel.

In terms of age there was a significant imbalance between the age ranges. Only one respondent (3.4%) was aged under twenty five; three (10.3%) were aged between 25-34 years of age; five (17.2%) were aged 35-44, whilst fourteen (48.3%) were aged between 45-54 and six (20.7%) were aged 55-64. These figures replicate the findings of other LR evaluations carried out by Cowen et al. (2000), Ross (2000, 2001), Cutter (2003) Wood and Moore (2005) and Wallis et al. (2005).

Thus more than two-thirds of the respondents were aged between 45-64 years of age. This finding was also noted during the early stages of the research process as age could well have a bearing as to how and if this cohort of LRs have been able or not to connect with teachers. Subsequent research failed to show that age was a factor in terms of the LRs firstly, being able to carry out their role and responsibilities effectively and secondly, being able to engage with their colleagues.

The participants were asked how long they had been a teacher and not one had less than six years service. Four (13.8%) had been a teacher for 6-9 years; six (20.7%) had between 10-15 years service and nineteen (65.5%) had fifteen or more years service. These results along with those outlining the age range clearly indicate that the typical EIS LR can be described as a mature individual with a significant length of service behind them. This may well make them a more credible representative as they have experience as well as age on their side or it may well put off younger teachers from seeking advice due to the significant age gap between them due to the very same factors. However, no evidence emerged to indicate that the latter was a factor.

In terms of the sectors the participants worked in, there was an even split between the primary and secondary sectors with thirteen (44.8%) working in the former and fourteen (48.3%) in the latter. One respondent (3.45%) worked in both sectors and another (3.45%) in the independent sector in a special needs residential school. These results show that there is even coverage in both sectors but raises the question of whether these authority-based representatives have been able to cross sectoral boundaries and make in-roads into a different sector from the one they work in. This issue was pursued because if the LRs were unable to help colleagues from different sectors this could prove to be a significant obstacle to overcome and in part would negate their effectiveness as an LR. Evidence collated from the question and answer and consultation group sessions suggested that this was not a significant issue but a small number of LRs did indicate that in the main they were working within their own sectors because they understood the issues that concerned their colleagues; did not feel comfortable moving outside their sector in terms of knowledge and understanding of how other sectors operated and time was also an issue. Some of these factors were raised in relation to other issues and questions and will be dealt with in greater detail below.

The participants were asked how long they had been employed by their current organisation and not one of them had been with their school for less than two years. Four (13.8%) had been with their school for 3-5 years; five (17.2%) had been with theirs for 6-9 years whilst a further five (17.2%) had been working for their school for 10-15 years and the majority, fifteen (51.7%) had been working for their organisation for fifteen or more years. These results would indicate that the majority of the respondents had been with their organisations for a significant amount of time. Thus they should have a rapport with both colleagues and management that aids them at least within their own immediate environment in terms of being able to discharge their duties as LRs and also with colleagues in other establishments within their authority area as they had worked there for a significant period of time. However, as the evidence will show this has not always been the case.

The participants were asked how long they had been a member of the Institute and longevity was a significant factor. Not one of them had been a member for less than three years; two (6.9%) had been members for 3-5 years; a further two (6.9%) for 6-9 years; seven (24.1%) had been a member for 10-15 years, whilst the majority, eighteen (62.1%) had been a member for fifteen or more years. If nothing else these results indicate that the Institute meant something to the respondents and they were willing to volunteer to become LRs.

Choosing to Become a Learning Representative

The participants were asked if they had held any type of trade union representative post before they had volunteered to become a LR. Fourteen (48.3%) stated they had held some type of position before, whilst the slight majority, fifteen (51.7%) had not held any position at all prior to volunteering to become a LR.

This is a key finding for a number of reasons. Firstly, compared to other LR evaluations the number of new activists recruited by the EIS far outstrips any other union. For example, Cowen et al. (2000: 10-11) found that 9% of their participants were new activists and more likely to be female, whilst Wallis et al.

(2005: 296-297) and the LRD (2006: 2) found that 27% and 36% respectively of their participants were new activists. Thus in a period spanning no more than five years the number of new activists has more than trebled if not quadrupled in most unions but the EIS dwarfs these figures by showing that the number of new activists it has recruited is five times the figure of just a few years ago and in most cases double what any other union has been able to achieve.

The key question at this early juncture was why did members that had held no type of position before suddenly become interested in this role? Particularly as they had been around a long time so to speak both in terms of their length of service and being a member of the Institute.

In the questionnaire the respondents were offered a range of options to state why and could choose more than one option. Thirteen stated it was for their own professional development and a further thirteen for their own personal development. Twenty one stated it was to improve the professional development of their colleagues, whilst ten wanted to become more involved in the EIS. Five of the respondents gave other answers as to why they volunteered and their comments are repeated below:

> *'Connect with other L Reps in Scotland...Following volunteering this has led to a lot more involvement in my professional association...Found trying to find info about Chartered Teacher and APL claims difficult. Therefore if I did others who are less aware would find it even harder... To become more involved in Education... To have an input into improving the quality of courses for teachers...Asked by Local Sec, as I was involved with Paisley Uni CT Modules prior to accreditation'.*

Thus it was fair to assume from the responses to this question that the key driver in volunteering to become a LR was about the personal and professional development of not only themselves but of their colleagues, rather than getting involved in the political nature of trade union representative work.

The personal records highlight three key reasons why the participants volunteered to become LRs. The first two are interlinked and the third will give trade unions and the EIS in particular something to think about. A number of participants stated that they became LRs because of their experiences linked to their CPD activities, particularly in relation to their involvement in Chartered Teacher (CT) courses. In turn, because of their experiences they wanted to help other colleagues who were embarking on their CT journey, as the following explanation clearly shows:

'I volunteered to be a ULR after setting up a peer support group as a student on the pilot EIS – University of Paisley Chartered Teacher modules. I had found the course materials particularly difficult and after being away from study for nearly nineteen years I found it was easier to meet up in local groups to discuss materials. I enjoyed supporting colleagues with their individual CPD and considered that being a ULR was a natural progression'.

However, as one participant pointed out, disillusionment also played a part in volunteering to become an LR. The participant stated:

'...I had always held the view that the courses for teachers should be of a high academic standard and should be applicable to the classroom-teaching situation. As my years in teaching rose the lack of continuum of learning became apparent and courses became repetitious and I stopped attending. I thought that by becoming a Learning Representative I would have an input to in-service course. I commenced the PGCOW [Post Graduate Certificate in Workplace Organisation] course in September 2001 and am now convinced that steps should be taken to make it as easy as possible for all teachers to study at postgraduate level'.

In terms of the third reason, a number of participants were interested or intrigued by the whole concept of becoming an LR as the following explanations show:

'I wanted to find out more about the whole concept of Learning Representatives within the EIS. Their role within the EIS was of interest to me. I also wanted the experience of becoming a Learning Representative'.

'...Local Association had nominated a learning rep ready for training, but he got early retirement. He spoke positively about the development that was about to take place. I was interested in doing the chartered teacher course myself, so was attracted to the possibility of supporting others'.

From the explanations given by the participants it is clear that volunteering to become a LR is in the majority of cases more about helping colleagues; having a genuine interest in the role rather than being fuelled by personal ambition and interest and this fits in with the research of Wood and Moore (2005: 11-13).

The other question of relevance was of those respondents that had held positions within the union, what type had they held and for how long? Of these nine had been a school representative; one had been a health and safety representative, whilst another had been a union representative in Canada. Seven of the respondents were committee members of their Local Association, with four out of the seven also having been a school representative. In terms of how long they had held positions, this ranged from 5-20 years, thus it is safe to assume that these respondents are dedicated representatives who have put the time in over the years and this evidence supports the findings of Cutter (2003) in relation to this issue.

The Training of the Learning Representatives

The aim of investigating the EIS LRs training delivered by the University of Paisley was not to evaluate the course itself but to determine whether it had given the LRs a solid platform from which as accredited LRs they could function within their authority areas. In terms of the course meeting its stated aims and objectives twenty one (72.4%) of the respondents stated that it had done so, whilst the remaining eight (27.6%) stated that it had done so to some extent. Thus it is fair to deduce that it did give the LRs a solid basis from which to proceed and this is backed up by a number of additional comments made by the participants such as:

> *'Thought the course was excellent...I feel it prepared me well for the job I do...It gave foundation for LR...Well structured/balanced course'.*

However, as some of the following comments indicate, there was a gap between theory and practice:

> *'It was very good – could be more links to actual practice and a section on securing CPD info and handling enquiries...Doesn't cover demands which are practical – more theoretical...A bit too general...Perhaps it could have been more specific but the role of learning rep was brand new – I was part of the first cohort'.*

The final comment is important as it is fair to argue that the initial intakes of LRs were "guinea pigs" for the initiative and the course and that the EIS and the University had nothing to go on in terms of previous experience or case studies from other unions. Despite having passed this course, the indications from some of these comments are that the LRs are having to learn on the job, which would be expected of a new initiative. In defence of the course and as was rightly pointed out by one of the participants above, it was the first running of it and no one could have envisaged all the issues and problems this type of representative would face in the field.

This line of examination was taken a step further when the participants were asked how relevant the training they had received was for the role they were performing as authority-based LRs. Four (13.8%) stated it was very relevant, whilst nineteen (65.5%) thought it had been relevant and six (20.7%) believed it had been slightly relevant. Thus for a significant minority, they could not turn theory into practice.

The evidence from the personal records suggests that the participants were very complimentary about the course run by the University of Paisley. The course was not only relevant but they also found it to be a positive and enlightening experience that gave them new skills that they could utilise in their role as a LR and in the classroom. They felt the course was well structured and run and enjoyed studying (particularly on-line) as for some was the first time they had done so for many years. The Paisley team both individually and collectively was praised for their efforts and for making the whole learning experience worthwhile. The views of the participants show that they feel that through the course they have been given a solid basis from which they can build and develop themselves as LRs as the following statements indicate:

'... The course enabled me to enhance my knowledge and skills in assertiveness techniques, stress management, social styles and to add the skills necessary for mentoring and counselling. I learned to match the needs of the individual with the needs of the organisation and I studied adults as learners. All of these I have used as a Learning Representative. I found the course extremely useful and I have revisited the course materials from time to time in order to deal with specific members' problems'.

'... There is much I have learned, especially in the realms of interpersonal skills, and the educational psychology of adults, that would have simply remained unknown to me. A fair bit has found direct application within my daily classroom teaching of secondary pupils, and formed part of a successful APL claim towards CT status'

'...I would only really support this criticism with regard to some of the case studies which appeared rather false & contrived, however, I was part of the first cohort and would like to think any weaknesses would have been addressed in

the future'.

Bernard McLeary (2005) states that one of the most positive aspects in relation to the LRs initiative is e-learning. He felt that the LRs are '...walking the talk'; using modern approaches to learning which in turn models what the profession wants to do and the LRs are not learning in the old didactic way.

EIS Support for the Learning Representatives

The participants were asked how often they sought guidance or support from EIS headquarters staff and officials and the answers seem to point to the fact that guidance and support was sought on an irregular basis. Only one (3.5%) respondent stated they used this service once a week; eight (27.6%) stated that they used it once a month; seven (24.1%) used it every three months, whilst three (10.3%) used it every six months and ten (34.5%) respondents gave other explanations. These included the following:

> *'Depends on the issue as well...I have also used the L.Rep website to get advice from other L.Reps... Whenever needed... As and when required, all queries are dealt with quickly and ably...Haven't required guidance so much recently but did when I was starting as a LR...Have yet to seek guidance with an LR query...Every other week sometimes two or three times...Only when required or during Learning Rep meetings...Between once a month/once every 3 months... Rarely...Should be more frequent but constrained by lack of time and volume of work...As required'.*

The logical conclusion from these answers is that the LRs are not dependent on the EIS national officers and officials for continuous guidance and support and are quite self-sufficient once they are up and running. It may also indicate that not many of their colleagues are coming to seek advice and guidance or have difficult problems. These issues were examined further and will be expanded upon in the next chapter.

The participants were asked what issues they had sought

guidance and support over and a number were highlighted more than once. These included time-off; parameters of the role in relation to the Local Association and general Chartered Teacher issues. The queries were dealt with in the main by e-mail communication, sometimes by a verbal discussion with officials and officers and occasionally through the dedicated website.

In terms of how effective this guidance and support has been, the participants seem very satisfied with the service they have received. Ten (34.5%) stated it was extremely effective; another ten (34.5%) stated it was very effective; six (20.7%) stated it was quite effective and there were no answers from three of the participants. This indicates that the EIS headquarters staff are servicing the LRs efficiently and effectively.

I would argue that the LRs are satisfied with the service they receive because of the time and effort put in, particularly by the key national officials involved with the LRs, notably, Lyn McClintock, Simon Macaulay and Veronica Rankin. I base this on my observations; the regular meetings organised for LRs where issues are aired and discussed; the development of tools for the job such as the dedicated LRs website, the LRs handbook, protocol and standards and the regular coverage LRs receive in the Institute's magazine – *Scottish Educational Journal.* In addition, I believe the manner in which Lyn McClintock took on her job in the first instance laid the foundations for a promising beginning to the LRs initiative as she describes below:

> *'…I went out to meet the LRs to get to know them and to give them some assistance in getting started in the role. I managed to meet up with all but one of them. I think that going out to meet the LRs face-to-face was very important – it has helped to build up the good rapport I have with them, from their point of view, it put a face to the name of the person allocated to work on this project on a full-time basis. My appointment was an indication of how important the EIS believes the project is and also reflected how fast the*

project was growing, even at that [early] stage' (McClintock, 2005: 1).

She goes on to state that:

> *'...sometimes I have fulfilled almost a counselling role – giving support and encouragement to LRs. There is a lot of e-mail contact and I have also spent a lot of time going out to meet current LRs...the current LRs who I've met with on a regular basis...seem to find this very supportive and I think it helps them to sit down and talk about how they are feeling – whether this is where they have not found the Local Association Secretary particularly helpful or supportive or where they find that their head teacher is not being supportive despite time off being agreed at authority level or where they find some of their colleagues appear to resent them being allocated time out of school'.* (McClintock, 2005: 3).

The participants were asked how often they utilised their dedicated website and the answers make for interesting reading. Ten (34.5%) used it once a week; another ten (34.5%) used it once a month; two (6.9%) once every three months, whilst another two (6.9%) every six months and five (17.2%) gave the following explanations:

> *'Every 2 weeks...Sometimes more than others depending on my free time...Occasionally...Not on a regular timescale... Have not used it much in the past but hope to do so more in the future...Variable – I try once/week but sometimes miss several weeks – depending on other work pressures'.*

The explanations clearly indicate that such a valuable tool was being under-used and this is a concern. As indicated above it seems that time pressures contributed to the under-utilisation of this resource. A guide as to why this resource was not being utilised comes in the form of the following comments made by some of the respondents:

> *'Now looking at it quite frequently, but only in the last month or so...I look at it a lot, but rarely post. I don't feel I have much worth adding yet...Should use it more often...*

The support given generally to the L.R.s by H.Q. staff is of a very high standard...I run the Dundee Learning Rep Website @www.dundeelearningrep.org.uk... Can't get online currently don't know password but generally I would utilise when the situation demanded...But usually when time allows. Time a significant restraint/constraint. Willing to carry out duties in free time, but other local authority union responsibilities and school based responsibilities a higher priority...Have trouble getting on to it...Password won't work. Sometimes I gave up instead of seeking more advice'.

Thus a multitude of answers and a sense that the site was not user friendly. This aspect was explored further as was that of certain LRs using their initiative and setting up local LR websites. Based on my observations of the website; the above comments made by the LRs and the concerns of national officers at the EIS' headquarters a process was set in motion (by Lyn McClintock and Veronica Rankin) to upgrade and reform the LRs' website. Subsequent meetings with LRs and observation of how the website was being utilised indicated that the LRs have few if any complaints about the website and are using it on a more frequent basis.

This chapter explored the demographic profile of EIS LRs and the reasons why they have volunteered to take on this role; the support and training they have received and how they are viewed by the key stakeholders. The next chapter interprets and develops Ball's (1993) policy trajectory and Bowe et al's. (1992) model by analysing the impact of the ULRs policy.

6

Obstacles and Prospects for Learning Representatives

Introduction

This chapter deals with the experiences of the LRs following the successful completion of their training. It examines their relationships with key operational stakeholders; obstacles they have encountered; dealing with colleagues and their interaction with colleagues. It also highlights the experiences of the LRs in order to analyse the effectiveness and impact of the LRs at an operational level.

Learning Representatives Experiences of Being Accepted by their Local Association

Overall the local associations have been welcoming and supportive of the LRs. In some cases they have invited the LRs to be members of the committee and a standing item on agendas. This clearly shows that at local level the LRs are becoming embedded within the structure of the EIS and have their own distinct identity. In a few cases this has been made easier because the LRs have held significant office within their local associations, notably the positions of Chair and Secretary.

However, in a number of cases the experiences of the LRs with their local associations have not been as positive as the following statements indicate:

> *'My LA has been welcoming, but don't actually understand what I do or what to do with us. And the LA chairman keeps referring to THE Learning Rep when there are 3 of us! Lyn* [McClintock] *has been invited to speak to them, and while they are welcoming I think that they are in need of guidance.*

They have come some way towards negotiating time off for us'.

'My experience of the Local Association has been mixed there is in my view a reluctance to accept the true value of the Learning Representative and an attitude that since there has been little call for this type of service why are we creating another job when we find it difficult to recruit people to the executive and as school representatives. I joined the local association to both establish local links and establish a channel of communication'.

The issue of local associations negotiating time-off for the LRs cropped up on a number of occasions and it was indicated that at times it has caused friction between the officers of the local association and the LRs, as the former are uncertain of the exact nature of an LR and how much time they require to fulfil their roles and responsibilities.

Lyn McClintock (2005: 1) sheds some light on this when she describes what the situation was like when she first approached the local associations to help the national officers negotiate facilities and time-off for the LRs. She states:

'...I met with some resistance from a few of the Local Association Secretaries – there appeared to be some resentment of the fact that they had not been allowed to choose who would be an LR and there was even a question mark with one or two over the necessity for LRs. In the same way that we had to break down barriers with Directors of Education and CPD Co-ordinators we were also having to do this with some of our own Local Associations – I don't think some people were too enamoured of my persistence in chasing them to negotiate time off as they did not understand the role itself or the significance of the role. One of the Local Associations, after several months of e-mail discussions did move to get time off and, not only that, but started to invite the LR to attend Local Association meetings and report on her activities. They also advertised her contact details within the newsletter. This

was a huge turnaround and I think a significant one'.

The acceptance of the LRs is key to the success of the EIS' LRs initiative and in the light of the evidence above the Institute will need to think how it formalises the LRs within its structures.

Learning Representatives Relationship with their own Institution

The participants indicated that overall they have a positive relationship with their institutions, senior management and colleagues. In the main head teachers have been positive and supportive of this development and can see the benefits it can bring in CPD terms for their staff. Colleagues of the LRs have also welcomed them in their new role and as with senior management can see the benefits of having an LR close by to help them with their CTS development. However, the issue of time-off was highlighted by a number of the LRs as having caused problems with their institutions.

The following comments are indicative of the situation highlighted above:

> *'My HT doesn't understand my role and has been physically unable to provide time off since February 2nd. She's on the big Local Authority CPD committee and I think that the union – therefore us – are seen as a pain in the neck. My LA hates us having time off, and indeed has made it difficult for us. The CPD committee has EIS reps, who are not trained learning reps and this undermines my argument with the "school" that I am a trained Union official who has important work to do within the world of CPD. My HT does however accept that CPD is vital and pushes people towards the institution based LR in training and towards the newly established team within the authority – who are again very nice but don't know what to do with us. It would seem however that they are starting to accept that we know a wee bit about the topic'.*
>
> *'Colleagues accepted and indeed promoted my role*

(incidentally, there is a high uptake of CT training in my establishment). HT values my teaching, so would prefer it if I didn't have time off for meetings and duties, but also is very positive about CPD, so is willing to let me carry out my duties'.

'Within my own institution, I felt I would gain more respect and momentum should I be discreet in my role of Learning Representative. Many teachers were very bitter about McCrone and diminishing PT posts were ready to attack the new structures. I did place a poster in the staff room and I realised advertising of the role was going on in other areas i.e. SEJ journal and TES. Occasionally teachers would ask me about the role. The Head teacher appeared supportive and recognised the role suggesting I take a place on the school CPD committee. When the Local Authority granted time off (½ day a week) for LR duties this was fine although it was a different matter, negotiating time off in school as a Learning Representative for meetings as this was met with resistance and a request that the meetings are highlighted a year in advance!!! Nonetheless within the last month or so things have been turning around. Aspiring Charter teachers in the school where I work have come for advice on their position regarding APL and courses in relation to Charter Teacher. I feel in my own institution that I have a role as the EIS Learning Representative and am someone that can be relied on to offer credible advice'

The evidence above should give all the stakeholders in Scottish education cause for concern as ULRs are enshrined in law and have certain minimum statutory rights. In addition the negative actions outlined above not only go against the letter and the spirit of the law they also go against the letter and spirit of the *McCrone Agreement* and the partnership approach to lifelong learning that all the major stakeholders in the Scottish education system have signed up to.

Learning Representatives Experiences of Being Accepted by Head Teachers

Whilst, the LRs may have been accepted by their own institutions and head teachers, a different story emerged at LR meetings and consultation groups. They highlighted a non-connection with many schools in their authority area and anecdotally it seemed that many in the Scottish education system were still not aware of LRs and their role. Jim O'Brien (2005) adds to the debate by stating there is significant tension at local level in schools as '...Head teachers have not been prepared to deal with the new collegial approaches post-McCrone'. He went on to state that head teachers '...might just tolerate LRs because they are there or head teachers perceive them as no real threat' and from his experience '...Head teachers have not talked about LRs – their concerns are about collegiality, the effects of down-sizing and the 35 hour week'. Thus, it is fair to surmise that LRs are way down the list of priorities and concerns of head teachers and may go some way to explaining the lack of positive feedback from the LRs in this area.

Bernard McLeary (2005) shed further light on the comments of Jim O'Brien by stating that firstly, he knew from his own local authority that there was suspicion of the LRs. One of the reasons was at the same time as LRs were coming onto the scene more negotiating processes were being introduced and head teachers were not used to negotiating with groups of trade union teachers and they lumped the LRs in with the representatives they would have to negotiate with. Secondly, heads questioned what the role of the LR would be in relation to brokering a relationship with the CPD member of the senior management team in terms of promoting CPD for the school and the individual. Thirdly, questions were being asked as to where the two roles fit in within a school and where they apart or could they work together? Hence the suspicion because they did not know but Bernard McLeary did point out that this was a slightly historical overview and matters may have moved on for the better.

Obviously, problems still exist and based on this evidence I decided that in order to analyse how deep-seated this problem was a number of head teachers in primary and secondary schools would be contacted by phone and asked at least one and possibly two questions. The first was if they knew what a LR is and if they answered in the affirmative then they were asked what they thought a LR's role and responsibilities are.

Their responses make for interesting reading. 15 out of the 16 (93.8%) primary heads responded and of those 10 (62.5%) stated they knew what a LR is, whilst 5 (31.3%) stated they did not. This was in contrast to the secondary heads (all of whom participated in the survey) where there was exactly a fifty-fifty split in the answers.

Overall, 18 (56.3%) of the participants stated they knew what a LR is, whilst disturbingly for the EIS, 13 (40.6%) did not know what a LR is. If this is replicated across Scotland, then the EIS message has failed to get through. This is even more disturbing when taking into account that the overwhelming majority of head teachers contacted where EIS members and that in Scotland, other specific head teachers' trade unions represent a significant number of heads.

The overwhelming majority of the heads that answered in the affirmative, where also able to describe what the role and responsibilities of a LR are. For example the following two primary heads stated that:

> *'Their role is to try and make teachers aware of courses and in-service training that is available to them and how they can enhance their careers through learning'*

> *'A learning rep is principally concerned with issues around learning and teaching and can offer advice on these issues. Whereas, an EIS rep is concerned with conditions of service'.*

Whilst another two had quite specific views on the LRs as

the following comments show:

'LRs are there to be a support mechanism for teachers on appropriate CPD opportunities/activities and for their CPD time. I have a concern that if LRs do not know the Development Plan in each school – which they [presumably the schools] want teacher CPD linked into – teachers could go off at a tangent. I think LRs need to speak to meetings of head teachers to explain their role and also to clarify that they are not trying to replace CPD Co-ordinators'.

'LRs are there to advise members on CPD particularly in relation to Chartered Teacher. I believe that LRs have set a good example by being prepared to undertake CPD themselves [i.e.] the course to become an LR. I think that the EIS having LRs is very positive and worthwhile. I have a couple of teachers in my school undertaking Chartered Teacher who have contacted the East Renfrewshire LR and received great support from her'.

The secondary heads that answered in the affirmative were also very positive in their answers to what a LR does as the following comments show:

'To advise and support teaching staff and EIS members about pedagogical issues surrounding educational developments particularly the issues linked to The Teaching Profession for the 21st Century'.

'An EIS trained individual who is there to offer advice and support to colleagues on CPD routes to either Chartered Teacher or for other reasons and also supports advice on approved courses such as those offered by Napier University I think'.

This last participant asked me if I was surprised that he knew what a LR was. This is an indication that there are still a large number of individuals in the Scottish education system who do not know what a LR is and does.

This is backed up by some of the answers to this survey, most disturbingly from those who claimed to know what a LR is. One of the respondents from the primary sector stated that a LR was '...trained to work with the Authority and that there should be one in every school' and admitted that she was not sure if she had mixed this up with the "Better Behaviour, Better Learning" initiative. Whilst another from this sector stated that a LR was there to '...take forward learning in the school clusters in relation to IT skills'.

In the secondary sector, the positive answers should also give cause for concern as the following answers show:

> *'We do not have a LR in East Ayrshire. They will have some sort of role with the local authority in relation to consultation on curricula activities. They will be the voice of the teachers. I am confused in terms of the overlap between the Secretary of the local association and the LR in terms of their roles'.*
>
> *'I have not had any personal dealings with them and I am not clear about what their role is'.*
>
> *'I am aware broadly that they have some sort of role giving advice to teachers about learning methodologies. I have a question as a head teacher as to where learning representatives fit in to other CPD roles in schools and roles where people are helping teachers develop learning and teaching'.*
>
> *'Not a clue but I have had no information on them sent to me'.*

The fact that almost 41% of the respondents did not know who LRs were must be of concern, particularly as their negative answers included such phrases as '...not a clue' and '...no idea'. It also begs the question as to where this leaves the partnership approach to lifelong learning, so clearly set out by all the major stakeholders in the Scottish education system.

Learning Representatives Experiences of Being Accepted by their Local Authority

The situation with local authorities is a mixed bag and the evidence suggests that there are significant difficulties for a number of the LRs as the following statements indicate:

'The authority is a nightmare! First they didn't want us to get time off, now they exclude us from things – but they have given us a wee den. This reflects the council's current position towards teachers in general and is not personal. I think it will take a long time before they accept us'.

'The Local Authority always recognised the role of the Learning Representative in principle. They agreed to time off for meetings and other duties on a "when needed" basis but emphasised as a teacher the needs of the school came first. CPD being a "tick box" exercise to most teachers in the early stages no time was given or considered needed except for the meetings held three times a year with other EIS Learning Representatives'.

'The Education Authority who have their own network of CPD coordinators formally acknowledge us but are essentially suspicious of everyone who may exercise any autonomy in this area regardless of any commitment to partnerships & providing a service to both members & CPD Coordinators'.

Lyn McClintock (2005: 2) elaborated further on this issue as follows:

'To assist in making Directors of Education and CPD Co-ordinators more aware of the role of LRs either Simon Macaulay or Veronica Rankin attended meetings of both explaining the role and how essential it was that the LRs were allocated specified time off to carry out the role. There appeared to be misconceptions initially in both these groups of what Learning Representatives were – they thought that it was

going to be a negotiating role and that this was another layer of the union they would be required to negotiate with'.

Bernard McLeary (2005) concurred with this view and believes that there are a number of issues related to LRs that are a cause for concern from a Director of Education perspective. Notably, the lack of clarity about the long-term objectives for LRs and he felt the LR scheme is still a "wait and see" innovation. He went on to state that from his neutral stance he was of the opinion that local authorities were suspicious of LRs. He sensed that there is some conflict because anything that is connected with a trade union has a history to it and went on to give the following example based on one of the training days he helped to run at the LTS' headquarters. He was giving an update on a curriculum issue and an EIS LR took exception to this in relation to the trade union and workload aspects of it. As he pointed out this was not the purpose of the day, it was just about giving an update and that was all. The LTS on that day was not selling the curriculum changes, it was not advocating the changes or promoting them, it was just giving information. He felt that the representative was basically giving a pay and conditions response and if this response is replicated at local authority level this will lead to role confusion.

However, a LR at a question and answer session warned that representatives need to be careful that they are not sucked into partnerships with local authorities who in turn end up defining the LRs role. This suspicion that LRs have of local authorities' activities and motives in relation to CPD and themselves was expanded upon at this session. One LR stated that her authority was putting CPD courses online so staff could access all courses on offer and not those filtered by management. To which another LR based in a different authority argued that local authorities put CPD online because it is cheap and fulfils their obligation and they are not bothered whether teachers take up courses or not.

These responses again put the partnership approach to

teachers' professional development in the spotlight, as historical precedent and lack of knowledge and trust on both sides at the operational level are proving to be barriers to the LRs working effectively on behalf of their colleagues and the education system.

Learning Representatives Relationship with Local Authority and School CPD Advisers

The responses to this issue were again mixed with some positive and negative observations but as with the previous issue a number of the representatives indicated that the relationship with their Local Authority and CPD advisers are tenuous in a number of cases as the following comments show:

> *'The school CPD advisors have not been particularly supportive. However at authority level they have been useful in referring members with a view to providing support to particular concerns'.*
>
> *'As I have had very little time out – 3 x 2½ hour blocks – I have yet to build up real relationships with CPD teams outwith my school...I am on the CPD and FSS committees (Framework for Staged Support). Our CPD co-ordinator is an establishment LR in training and we work as a very close unit'.*

Lyn McClintock (2005: 2) sheds further light on these comments as she observed that there:

> *'...was also suspicion and concern amongst some CPD Co-ordinators that the Learning Reps would take over their role. We had to explain to them that the LRs were added value to the CPD service already being provided by the authorities...A Frequently Asked Questions leaflet was drawn up and widely circulated to educate both people outwith and within the union on the role and benefits of LRs'.*

This attitude was confirmed by a LR at a question and answer session, who stated that CPD Co-ordinators in her local authority were fearful of losing their jobs due to the introduction of LRs. The LR had pointed out to them that the representatives are not a threat to them and that the co-ordinators should open the door to them. Another LR backed this statement up but added that LRs were not going to be accepted straight away and they needed to work at it to gain the acceptance and trust of others, particularly the stakeholders.

However, positive developments and initiatives were highlighted by a number of the participants as the following comments indicate:

> *'The Local Authority CPD Adviser is very helpful and pleasant. We meet regularly to discuss issues and keep up-to-date with developments in CPD. I have no contact with school CPD advisers yet'.*

> *'[The Local Authority]...has no advisers I work closely with the Quality Improvement Officer who manages CPD meeting her every 2 to 3 weeks. We have established an excellent working relationship. I am a member of the CPD Steering Group and attend meetings of School CPD Coordinators. I write the minutes for the Steering Group and the Coordinators' meetings. With School CPD coordinators I have established good communications by circulating minutes promptly, answering their queries and providing solutions to some of the CPD difficulties they have met as they learnt how to use the East Renfrewshire CPD web site, an online catalogue of courses and booking service. I am about to accompany the QIO on a pilot review of CPD in one of our schools'.*

> *'The council sees the benefits of working with the EIS in connection with learning reps and they suggested working with our advisory service, the teachers CPD working group and the whole council CPD (training and education) group'.*

The participant went on to indicate how he worked with

these various groups and the following example of working with the Advisory Service typified the positive relationship this participant had with his CPD colleagues:

> *'…I made contact with the head of the advisory service who organises all In-service training courses and was pleased to find that she was willing to work with me in supporting teachers reach a full CPD program. The only problem that I have still to overcome is that of being allowed access to the school CPD coordinators'.*

This final point of trying to build up a relationship or rapport with CPD Advisers/Coordinators seems to be a recurring problem with the participants as highlighted at the beginning of this section and typified by the following response from another participant:

> *'So far, two out of four of us have been "allowed" a 10-minute address to two different groups (out of 5) of CPD coordinators. Some appeared genuinely interested in what we had to say. "Are you available to visit?" "Do you charge for advice?" But the directorate seem less enthusiastic'.*

These comments as with those concerned with the local authorities clearly highlight a non-connection between the LRs and the operational stakeholders and as mentioned previously brings into question the partnership approach to the professional development of teachers. Particularly, as the strategic stakeholders have clearly stated that the EIS LRs have an important role to play in this area. The key problem is the suspicion of LRs and lack understanding as to their role and responsibilities which has led to a major barrier being created between the co-ordinators and the LRs.

Obstacles Learning Representatives Have Faced

The participants highlighted a number of obstacles that have significantly hindered their ability to carry out their roles and responsibilities as LRs. Eight (57.1%) of the respondents (who produced personal records) highlighted the issue of time-off as the major obstacle as the following statement indicates:

'...Main one has not been having a permanently negotiated time off allowance – has tended to go from term to term, with LA Secretary having to negotiate with the Director of Education each term. This has made setting up a system of support for teachers more difficult'.

It was clearly indicated that very few teachers had contacted the representatives for advice and guidance and the following statement is indicative of the current situation faced by EIS LRs:

'...to date the number of members who have contacted me has been in the low tens and most of these have been in connection with the CT program. I have sent out publicity material to all schools but feel that if I want to make more of an impact I must first work with the CPD coordinators and then secondly, get out to schools and let teachers know what I look like and what I can do to help them. Visiting schools' will be a priority this year since it is only by being seen will people contact me. (The main reason that I think I get very few enquiries is that within my authority we have a very well structured CPD set-up and most people get access to courses through our advisory service.)'.

Other obstacles that were highlighted by a number of the participants and relate to the two highlighted above were actually having the time to act as an LR, as no cover was provided; the seemingly negative attitude of the Local Authority towards the LRs and what they were trying to achieve; the inability to create a constructive working relationship with CPD coordinators and accommodation in terms of having a dedicated space from which to carry out LR activities free from interruption and interference. Indicative of the problem of obstacles that the EIS LRs face is that less than a handful of respondents indicated explicitly or otherwise that they had not faced any obstacles whilst performing their duties as LRs and they did not further elaborate on this answer.

Lyn McClintock (2005: 3) backs up these claims as she states that a:

> '*...lot of time has been taken up with discussions with the LRs regarding their time off, the role etc. and liaising with the necessary people to try and secure the time off. Even when time off has, we believe, been agreed there have been some local difficulties for some LRs and this takes a lot of time and effort both in relation to myself and in discussions with Simon and Veronica.*

Jim O'Brien (2005) is of the opinion that there are a number of obstacles and points out the following:

> '*Teachers not knowing about them* [LRs] *and being unaware of their roles. HEIs* [Higher Education Institutions] *have a limited awareness of LRs because of invitation to provide CPD details of courses etc., but it will be a conscious decision to work actively with them. The tensions between the employers and the EIS may not go away with regard to the LRs. LRs are geared to more individual needs rather than the system and individuals may play LRs off the organisation to pursue personal needs rather than the needs of the employer'.*

Bernard McLeary (2005) took another tack stating that in terms of obstacles faced, the situation of the LRs had to be looked at from a managing change perspective and that the LRs are part of a management of change process and the EIS has to recognise this. He felt that a lot of effort has been put into the development of LRs, for example, through the Paisley course and marketing publicity but what the EIS should be doing is selling what the LR is and does to all stakeholders and not just the teachers, and suggested that Directors of Education should be targeted for example. Bernard offered a personal observation that the EIS trade union view is that it expects change to happen because it has a new structure in place (the LRs) but they do not work at it as agents of change.

At a question and answer session one of the LRs felt that

the senior and line managers in schools could end up being the real barriers to CPD for a number of reasons with the most significant being the cost of CPD to schools. The LR went on to add that if managers are not to become barriers to CPD then they need the time and the training to deal with CPD effectively. The situation seems to be exacerbated by two further examples highlighted by two separate LRs. Firstly, the secondary sector is reluctant to take up CPD which makes the LRs jobs more difficult and secondly in Glasgow where the stance of the local authority is that there is no need for LRs because it believes it has a good CPD set-up.

These factors further highlight the lack of commitment to the partnership approach to professional development at the operational level and those who need to interact with the LRs at this level do not seem to have a clear understanding of what a LR is.

Learning Representatives Experiences in Dealing with their Colleagues

Overall the participants stated that their experiences with the colleagues who have contacted them (albeit on a limited basis) have been positive and rewarding and the LRs have been able to deal with the requests either immediately or as soon as they could get the information required by the member as highlighted by the following statements:

'Most experiences have been positive. I have visited schools and spoken to groups of teachers. Any queries I couldn't deal with then have been answered in due course. The main problem is the fact that members are not using the Learning Representative services. I'm not sure if this is down to a lack of awareness amongst colleagues, or down to the fact that, like any other union service, members don't want to use the union until they feel disadvantaged or threatened'.

'Communication is by e-mail, a few phone calls and sometimes I am stopped in the street. The busiest times have been in Jan/Feb when many schools hold their Review and Development interviews. In most cases the queries are about the Review and Development system and what constitutes a CPD activity and clarification is all that is needed. On a couple of occasions where members were being bullied into CPD they did not wish I passed to the Local Association Secretary. I have responsibility for aspiring Chartered Teachers and have held meetings as needed and communicated on a "how are you doing?" basis each semester. I have visited schools to speak to staff about the CT programme and have given advice on how to make an APL (Accredited Prior Learning) claim using my portfolio as an example. I recently held an evening where Rosa Murray of the GTCS spoke about the GTCS accreditation route and the universities had stalls. All of these have resulted in positive feedback.

I am about to work with a teacher who has difficulty with classroom management and intend to help him devise an action plan to address this. This is being done at the request of the Local Association Secretary'.

'Until very recently, over the last two years, I have not had the opportunity to deal with colleagues with the exception of one or two who have asked what it is I do exactly. However recently there have been people approach me in relation to CT asking advice on the providers and APL. I was also taken aback when a colleague asking for advice became very emotional as she lacked confidence to take on a course. I believe my experience on the LR module did allow me to expect this and I have been successful in working with the teacher who is now enrolled in module one'.

However, as has been previously highlighted, there is significant concern that very few "punters" are coming through the door to seek assistance from the LRs and this is causing the LRs considerable worry and to a degree questioning their role. One LR stated that he was starting to feel quite frustrated by the lack of response from members despite putting on a lot of initiatives, for example, a CPD seminar that had a good attendance but not a lot of response afterwards. He stated that he felt it was '…like working in a vacuum' as he was (perversely) getting support from his local authority and the EIS at local and national level but not from the members.

This comment sparked a debate amongst the LRs at the meeting and a number of them put forward reasons why members were not coming forward to use the services of the representatives. One stated that they had a good working relationship with their CPD Co-ordinator but the members were not interested, they were apathetic and were not embarking on CT. Another LR put it down to workload and financial issues and was supported by a colleague who stated that it is a work-life balance issue and teachers are struggling to deal with their current workload, let alone contemplate further CPD. Whilst another pointed out teachers are not accessing CPD online, that CPD is on the back burner in many schools and '…it is easy for authorities to say courses are full when only 20 are allowed on a course and there are 5000 teachers!'.

The issues of when CPD is delivered, the content of CPD courses and the type of professional development that teachers should pursue where also highlighted as areas where the LRs are having problems engaging with members. One LR felt that CPD should not just be about courses and that other types of professional development should be recognised and they were supported by another LR who argued that there is a need to talk about personal rather than professional development. Whilst another was of the opinion that the "35 hours" is a tick box exercise and it is not what the teachers want in terms of CPD as many are undertaking this CPD merely from a contractual perspective. The LR went on to argue that professional development is becoming the schools' development and not the teachers' development and thus members are adhering to their school's development plan. It is fair to surmise that if this is the case and it is widespread in Scotland, this could negate the role of the LR to a degree.

This point was picked up by another LR who was of the view that far too many school managers are not genuinely interested in CPD or CPD is not made explicit enough and in turn this creates apathy. The LR felt that this was the case in the majority of schools and school management was happy with this situation, but it was the role of the LRs to get into schools that have this negative culture and change it.

This negative approach to CPD by teachers is not just anecdotal as two recent academic studies by Draper and Sharp (2006) and Connelly and McMahon (2007) back up the arguments and statements of the LRs. Janet Draper (formally of the University of Edinburgh and now Senior Lecturer and Fast Track Co-ordinator at the School of Education and Lifelong Learning, University of Exeter) who has studied CPD developments in great detail for a number of years elaborated on the findings of her study and the experiences and views of the LRs.

She stated that until relatively recently, CPD was not instilled as an integral part of a teacher's job; it is only in the last ten years that CPD has become part of practice and pre-McCrone a lot of formal professional development tended to be tied to school management rather than professional practice. Thus, there are a significant number of teachers who have not seen professional development as relevant to their needs (Draper, 2006). This in part can explain the low take-up of CPD and CT in particular but does not fully explain the apathy of the teachers that the LRs highlighted above.

In answer to that Janet Draper (2006) stated that post the *McCrone Agreement* from a financial perspective there was no point teachers going for CT if they had already been promoted and went on to add that by 15 years in the job teachers in the secondary sector were on the management rung, thus a significant number of them do not apply for CT. She went on to add that her research found that far more primary than secondary teachers are pursuing CPD and historically this was the case before CT was introduced.

Significantly, Janet Draper (2006) pointed out that many teachers cannot undertake CT because they need to be on the top point of the main pay grade scale and that the teachers who do undertake CT fall into two groups those who are enthusiastic and those who want to enhance their pensions. She went on to add that there is another group of teachers who want to sign up for further professional development but personal and domestic circumstances will not allow them due to having to look after children; elderly relatives; being a single parent and/or being part of a dual income family. These factors do not allow them the time to pursue professional development and for example, added to the dual income family, the job itself has become more intensified and there is too much (and much more) bureaucracy and accountability, which means they have no time and they are fed up.

Other factors were also highlighted by Janet Draper (2006) such as teachers who are parents also have a view that they want to be involved in their children's development and from Paterson's (1998) work that teachers are also civic activists, thus they see no real need to involve themselves in CPD. Of equal significance is that teachers have to pay for their CPD/CT courses which they are resentful of, particularly as if they were training to be a head teacher they would not have to pay (if they took this developmental route) and would in turn benefit financially.

She went on to add that Scottish teachers are suspicious of CT because the Scottish Executive is supportive of it; that they are naturally conservative and for example, will wait and see how CT will progress and how colleagues have coped with it before they take up opportunities such as CT. The situation is not aided by evidence that she has uncovered that micro-politics in schools are playing a part in the low take up of CT, as there is peer pressure not to take up CT with colleagues being critical of others for doing so. It has got to the point that some teachers are not telling people they are doing CT (Draper, 2006). This may well help to explain in part why teachers are not engaging with LRs on CPD and CT matters.

Interestingly, Janet Draper (2006) also highlighted the argument being put forward by some Scottish teachers that their own professional development is based on their own critical reflection on practice which they feel is a good way to develop. As she pointed out they say '...the most developing thing I do is my job'. She went on to state that this shows that CPD is absolutely core to their job and that a number of teachers have misunderstood what CT is about. Many think it is not rooted in practice but Janet Draper argues that this is not actually the case and it is the opposite. Again the issues highlighted here linked to those above may well help to offer a further part explanation as to the non-connection between the EIS LRs and their colleagues.

However, one LR has noted some positive developments in increasing contact with members and this has been a recent occurrence. The LR felt that the increase in contact with members was partially down to his photograph in the Institute's magazine which showed him graduating as a Chartered Teacher and a change of tactics on his behalf. He felt that initially he did not provide the information the members had required and he had addressed this. Since this change of tactic he has noted a change in attitude to CPD and that colleagues are now of the opinion that it is not only about professional development but also about teachers' personal needs.

The following chapter builds upon the findings in this chapter and Chapter 5 by taking Ball's (1993) policy trajectory and Bowe et al's. (1992) model a step further by examining how the EIS LRs role has developed and the potential for further development.

7

Moving Forward

Introduction

This chapter seeks to highlight how the role of LRs has developed and how they envisage it developing in the future. It also examines the personal and professional consequences of being a LR. The aim of this approach is to assess the relevance of LRs at the operational level in supporting their colleagues and being able to work in partnership with local authorities, schools and CPD Advisers.

The Effect Being a Learning Representative

Overall, the participants felt that becoming a LR has had a beneficial effect on them from both a personal and professional perspective. The experience has been an enjoyable one from the outset in terms of the University of Paisley course, which in turn has given them new skills as well as enhancing others they had. A number stated that it had opened a new world for them in a number of ways. It has fired up their enthusiasm for CPD not only from a personal perspective but also in helping others. It has introduced them to the world of trade union representation and the benefits of helping colleagues. It has also made them proud to be a LR and more confident in terms of greater participation in meetings, making public speeches and dealing with colleagues. It has given them a new found confidence and the ability to make action plans to enhance their role as LRs. The following statements are indicative of how the respondents felt on this issue:

> *'Being a ULR has broadened my horizons and has provided a detailed insight as to how councils formulate their CPD policies and how they perceive that they support*

this. Professionally it has provided an insight how to support colleagues to gain high quality CPD.

The CT programme and the ULR course have reinvigorated my personal teaching and how I relate this to the classroom, school and studies that have also monitored parents' perceptions. Before embarking on these studies I was very insular in my classroom and department'.

'The effect that being a Learning Representative has had on me has been major; it has allowed me to develop personally an understanding of how life long learning works and my own capacity to develop professionally in my understanding of teaching and learning for adults as well as children. I now have a much clearer view of how both the union and the educational system works.

'... The good initial training and very relevant follow up has given me a lot of confidence – much less hesitant to speak up at meetings. The training has given me confidence to either help immediately, or know where to go for information. It has also made me much more confident as I undertake the CT course, supported by the network of contacts that I have built up. I spoke at last year's EIS AGM in Dundee, and will speak at this year's AGM in Perth on issues related to CPD. I would never have pictured myself doing this in the past'.

A small number of the participants who wrote personal records made negative comments in relation to this issue and their comments make for interesting reading as the following selection will indicate:

'Professionally, I don't know yet as soon I will be interviewed for my Principal Teacher job due to an amalgamation of two schools. It will be interesting to see how a P.T. being given time off for union activities is viewed by a new head teacher. I also have aspirations to apply for DHT jobs soon and it will also be interesting to see if the Learning Representative

position will have to be sacrificed.

In some respects I feel that being a Learning Representative has also held me back. At the time that I was accorded the status of a Learning Representative, I was "upgraded" from PT Computing to a PT Business Education and Computing faculty. I have no Business Education background and there has been friction in prioritising time between Learning Representative duties and departmental responsibilities, i.e. becoming more knowledgeable about Business Education curriculum. Personally, I feel undervalued by the authority and members... but valued by the union at national level'.

'Holding the position of Learning Representative did cause problems initially with my own school's CPD coordinator as she was reluctant to allow me to attend requested courses and still has a tendency to stop my request for courses suggested for senior staff. I have had to fight to get on courses and have, at times had to talk with my head teacher about this. (My CPD coordinator knows that the appropriate target group is only put in as a guide and that courses are open to all interested staff – It is only the cost that is the possible block).

Although the above was/is still a problem I have been allowed to attend excellent courses arranged by the EIS on Media Awareness and on the working of LT Scotland. I have also been allowed to do as many after school courses as I like. It would appear that if my requested course is not run by our advisory service then it is much harder for me to get on it where as other staff can get on any course they like (preferred staff)'.

The positive comments are significant and bode well for the future of the EIS' LRs initiative and should be used partly to advertise to the role to prospective LRs; help develop the role of LRs through the University of Paisley course and adapted for presentations by LRs to other colleagues, particularly the quarterly LRs meetings.

Learning Representatives Developing their Role

The LRs responses to this issue were patchy with a number either not addressing this it at all, whilst others briefly dealt with it and some went into more detail. Of those who did comment the following key points emerged:

'Since August 2004 as the... Learning Representative I have been provided 1 day per week for duties. The time has been constructively used to support learning initiatives and in particular the Chartered Teacher programme... This has involved attendance at university and other CPD events. It has enabled information to be kept up-to-date to answer queries that offer reliable support for individual teachers'.

'I feel developing my role as an L.R. will be easier when the other two reps in training qualify/are accredited. The reason for these (sic) being that 3 people will have more exposure than one'.

'The local EIS secretary is negotiating time off from my teaching duties so that I can meet with teachers during breaks and be available to chat with them in their staff rooms. As well, I have attended two EIS local meetings to explain to members present my role as qualified Learning Representative. I have suggested that I be put on the agenda of each meeting of the Local [Association] so that I can reach more members and define my role further to them'.

One of the respondents set out how she planned to develop her role in table form. The respondent had objectives, tasks, success criteria, when the objective would be met by and a final section with additional notes. The key objectives were as follows:

'1. To develop a working office and a data base system for Learning Rep.

2. To promote CPD within the education community. Collaboration with EIS, EIS Learning

Reps, EIS members, LA, GTC, university providers and other appropriate agencies in relation to CPD.

3. To promote CPD and Lifelong Learning to EIS members in Clackmannanshire.

4. Research and sharing of good practice'.

Finally, another participant sought to develop his role along similar lines to the previous respondent as follows and it is interesting to note the importance of having a working space from which to operate and creating and maintaining databases are again highlighted:

'Develop better recording systems to allow me to keep track of everything that I have been asked to do and keep details of courses available from all providers of CPD. I would like to find an office where I can be contacted at and also have space to leave contact details easily available for anyone who requests them'.

These examples not only show that the LRs are dedicated to their role but are not content to sit back and do the minimum. They are prepared to think about their role and examine ways in which they can improve the service they provide for the benefit of their colleagues. This is a significant point and one that should not be underestimated and in turn be brought to the attention of the operational stakeholders at local authority and school level who are suspicious of LRs and have a distinct lack of understanding as to who they are and what they do.

Learning Representatives Initiatives

The responses of the participants clearly indicate that they have been pro-active and innovative in their role as LRs as the fol*lowing comments indicate:*

'During my time I have been involved in the following activities:

- *As part of the... CPD Working Group, collaborating in the development of a proforma for the PRD process that involves the recording of CPD opportunities with* a *view to monitoring the 35-hour commitment to CPD as outlined in the McCrone agreement. This involved the creation and redrafting of materials, developing exemplars and verifying the materials against the National Framework documents.*

- *Created and developed a website for... teachers.*
- *Attending regular monthly meetings with... the CPD Co-ordinator.*
- *Giving a presentation on the role of the Learning representative to staff development co-ordinators across all education sectors.*
- *Giving a presentation on the role of the Learning Representative to staff in secondary schools.*
- *Arranged a primary school visit to discuss the Chartered Teacher programme.*
- *Answered queries by teachers surrounding Chartered Teacher and CPD in general.*

My main development has been the creation and development of a website focussing on the following areas:

- *Standards For Learning Representative*
- *PDR/CPD For... Teachers*
- *Information For Other Learning Representative, including the aforementioned presentation'.*

'Initiatives I have tried to encourage uptake, have been letters to establishment representatives, posters, e-mails, presentations to staff rooms and personal visits'.

'When I was doing Module One I organised a local support group for others doing the course. Many found this beneficial as it was face-to-face and I was able to answer queries and assist with using Blackboard'.

'To date the most successful initiative was providing the local Authority CPD coordinator with the idea then helping

with planning a successful CPD open day in May 2005. Early next term I will visit schools in the area to talk to teachers about my role and how I can be of assistance to them. I am also keen to distribute a Needs Survey as I feel the responses will help target what members want from the Learning Representative. Additionally encourage other members to be in touch'.

As has been previously highlighted the dedication and ingenuity of the LRs is clear for all to see and they work not for self-promotion but to help their colleagues better themselves from a professional perspective.

Learning Representatives Perceptions of their Future Role

The participants had firm ideas as to how their role will and should develop in the future and it is fair to surmise that they are positive and upbeat as to how this can be achieved as the following comment indicates:

'The Chartered Teacher programme, in particular, opens up real possibilities for collaboration, which will maximise the professional development of teachers and lead to real benefits for children. It is therefore considered that further opportunities can be developed to ensure that this work is a complementary service in the Renfrewshire teacher support network'.

It is clear from this comment that partnership is seen as the way forward and that this LR does no regard himself as a threat to the Local Authority or the CPD co-ordinators, but as previous comments have clearly indicated there is a reluctance amongst local authorities and CPD co-ordinators to work with the EIS LRs for the benefit of the teaching profession in Scotland. This point is backed up by the following comment:

'In future I hope to get time out, to be involved a lot more with CPD developments within the authority and to be more active in being able to assist in finding funding etc

for members. I believe I have a valuable role to play – it's just going to take a while for people to understand that'.

Meanwhile another respondent has created a spreadsheet with tasks, action points, the person responsible and timescales in relation to future development. The main tasks he has set himself and fellow LRs in the short term are as follows:

> *'1. Create a publication that informs members of the role of the Learning Representative to be issued by [the Local Association].*
>
> *2. Prepare presentation on the role of a Learning Representative for staff on request.*
>
> *3. To contact staff via an area for CPD on the First Class system.*
>
> *4. Update the [Local Association] EIS CPD website regularly.*
>
> *5. Retrieve and gather information on CPD opportunities and where appropriate, evaluations.*
>
> *6. Research latest CPD developments.*
>
> *7. Update [the local] EIS Learning Representative website to include section on Chartered Teacher Programme.*
>
> *8. Create section specific to Chartered Teacher Programme.*
>
> *9. Create an electronic discussion group restricted to those on Chartered Teacher programme.*
>
> *10. Organise local support groups'.*

In the longer term the respondent tellingly states that:

'...I have to think long and hard about the conflict between the duties of a Learning Representative and my career aspirations in management. A head teacher has advised me that I will soon have to make a decision to go down a "union" route or "management" route. At present I feel that I am setting up support structures that others can perhaps follow on and maintain in the future.

At the moment I'm happy doing what I can do, but the

level of interest from members... has really been disappointing, and quite frankly makes me wonder why we bother. I feel that I've done quality work and got no recognition from it by the members – the people who matter. The only thing that keeps me going is the feeling at the back of my mind that the work we are doing is worthwhile.

Moreover, there is no point in being a Learning Representative if the time off implications are not addressed. At the moment I am totally exasperated by the authority paying lip service to time off, although the feeling is usually cyclical. Come the next meeting of Learning Reps this feeling will dissipate and I usually become more energised'.

These final statements have not been made in isolation as the following respondent's comments show:

'The role of the Learning Representative has still to find acceptance in my area. I would hope to see it develop as both a support to union members, as a bridge between members and the CPD coordinators and planners in LA. There should also be a link to colleges, universities and other CPD providers'.

The above comments may well seem negative and justifiably so but other LRs are upbeat about the future as the following comments indicate:

'I see the role developing in the future as there will be 3 of us for the City from June 2005 and 3 heads are better than 1 for thinking up initiatives. As people start going through the C.T. programme more people will become involved and more people will ask for advice. Unlike other Local Authorities where the CPD opportunities are not well organised I feel because of this the L.R.s will not necessarily have a direct influence on the City's CPD programme. However, if omissions are "flagged up" to us, then we would pursue that as we are in place to support the membership'.

'I should like to think that as EIS members become more aware of LR's that there will be more demand for my services.

There has been a lot of publicity about LR's in the union journal and on the website and I hope this will encourage more members to think about their CPD and seek help from their LR'.

'The EIS initiative to train Institution based Learning Representatives is an exciting one. It will free up Authority based Learning representatives to more fully assist teachers in schools who do not have a CPD co-ordinator. As well, the Authority based Learning Representative will have the role of liaising both with the Local Authority and the School based Learning Representative'.

'I hope my role as Learning Representative will grow. As it becomes evident to teachers, they are responsible for their own CPD I hope they will turn to me for advice and support when making decisions in relation to their careers. I would like to work with the Local Authority to ensure that all our members are give equal opportunities of quality CPD'.

However, this optimism is tempered by the response of another participant who states that:

'I have also proposed a meeting & agreed with the office bearers in the new session with regard to negotiating on time-off and other matters. If we can't move forward, the LR will effectively exist in name only with a very superficial role which involves simply signposting websites & other information. This would simply be a waste of time & opportunity'.

This final comment succinctly highlights the need for local authorities and senior school management to get to grips and understand the concept of LRs and what these representatives can do to help them implement successful CPD initiatives and schemes. Particularly, as Bernard McLeary (2005) states that the EIS LRs fit into what the LTS wants of communities of practice. The LRs are a community of practice based on being reflective practitioners and this is the modern role of a teaching trade union, which goes beyond the protection of terms and conditions of employment.

The answer may in part lay with the initiative pioneered in Aberdeenshire where the Council and the EIS have signed a Partnership Learning Agreement (Aberdeenshire Council and EIS, 2005). It can be regarded as a model of best practice as the Council clearly sets out its commitment to lifelong learning and CPD by working in partnership with the EIS and recognising the importance of LRs in this process. As the agreement states:

> *'The aims of both Aberdeenshire Council and Trade Union Learning Representatives and Advisers are therefore compatible and will be realised when all parties communicate, co-operate and share ideas, information and resources. Both parties are committed to the implementation of this agreement and will work together to ensure its success' (Aberdeenshire Council and EIS, 2005: 1).*

The agreement not only has a clearly defined purpose and set of principles it also lays out the rights and roles of LRs; responsibilities of the EIS and the Council; the roles of line managers and school CPD co-ordinators and the relationship between the Council's Corporate Development and Training Unit and the EIS LRs (Aberdeenshire Council and EIS, 2005: 2-6).

This approach is backed up by Wallis and Stuart (2007) who have examined a number of workplace learning agreements and point out that such agreements have a positive effect. Significantly, they state that in:

> *'...all the case study organisations, the development of a partnership based approach to learning, and the conclusion of learning agreements were made possible by the positioning of learning within a framework for mutual gains, and a recognition on the part of management that not only had the trade unions a significant role to play in attracting non-traditional learners and unskilled employees to learning activities, but that ULRs also represented a resource that*

was complementary to (rather than in competition with) the human resources/training function' (Wallis and Stuart, 2007: 8).

Wallis and Stuart (2007: 11-18) also highlight a number of positive outcomes of these agreements, particularly:

- Improving relations between management and the trade unions;
- Increasing opportunities for employees to undertake learning;
- Promoting equality of opportunity in relation to learning;
- Helping to improve employee morale through increased learning opportunities;
- Enlarging the internal pool of labour available to the organisations' human resources/training departments, for example ULRs either by helping them with training courses and in some cases taking up positions within these departments ;
- Generating business benefits for the organisations such as Investors in People accreditation;
- Increasing the potential for collaboration and more coordinated activities between trade unions;
- Increasing the potential for trade unions to increase membership.

This is how partnership in learning should work between employers and trade unions and one that should be noted by the other 31 local authorities in Scotland. Such agreements may well help to avoid a number of the issues and problems highlighted in this study.

The final chapter seeks to bring this book together by highlighting the key issues that have emerged from this study and makes a number of observations that stakeholders may wish to consider in order to realise the potential benefits of the LRs to all those involved in Scottish education.

8

Progress Through Partnership

Overview

The creation of the LRs initiative was a risk by the EIS as it took the Institute out of its "comfort zone" and into unknown territory from the perspective of a trade union that is primarily in existence to represent the collective bargaining interests of its members. However, the EIS was formed to look after the professional development needs of its members and its modern day commitment to this is its support of the *McCrone Agreement* (SEED, 2001); its partnership with the University of Paisley in relation to the delivery of CPD courses and the LRs initiative. The evidence presented in this book shows that overall it was worth the EIS taking this risk but there is work to be done by not only the Institute but by both strategic and operational stakeholders in the Scottish education system.

The first cohort of EIS LRs are a dedicated and enthusiastic group who are committed to the cause of teacher professional development and have demonstrated their initiative and resourcefulness when it has come to not only establishing themselves but also overcoming obstacles that have been put in their way either deliberately or inadvertently. The LRs do not rest on their laurels and are continually looking at ways of improving the service they provide to their colleagues. They are ably supported by the Institute itself that has appointed a dedicated officer to look after them; created a unique training course for them; a dedicated website; regular updates and meetings and a handbook.

These initiatives are of the utmost importance due to the significantly high level of new activists that have been recruited as LRs by the EIS. The fact that so many new activists have been recruited should not only be celebrated in terms of the EIS recruiting more than any other union proportionately but also that these representatives have volunteered because they have bought into the whole concept of CPD for teachers and believe they can positively help their colleagues.

The key strategic stakeholders in Scottish education, namely the Scottish Executive, General Teaching Council Scotland and Learning and Teaching Scotland not only openly support the LRs initiative but are committed to it. They recognise the benefits to the teaching profession of such representatives and that the LRs fit into the partnership approach to learning that all key stakeholders in Scottish education have signed up to. They also regard the LRs as integral to the success of the CPD element of the *McCrone Agreement* (SEED, 2001).

However, despite some promising developments, at the operational level of Scottish education the study has highlighted a number of issues and problems that could endanger the bi-partisan approach to lifelong learning and the effectiveness of the LRs to help their colleagues. The evidence presented demonstrates that there is a non-connection between the LRs and local authorities, CPD co-ordinators, school management, head teachers and teachers. This is in part due to historical adversarial relationships between the EIS and employers; a lack of trust and understanding of who and what LRs are and do amongst local authorities, CPD co-ordinators and head teachers and a continuing scepticism about the CPD benefits of the *McCrone Agreement* (SEED, 2001) amongst teachers.

From the perspective of the local authorities and head teachers there is a clear lack of understanding of who LRs are and what their role and responsibilities are. There has been a breakdown in communication between the EIS and these pivotal operational stakeholders. However, the situation is exacerbated by the local authorities and head teachers continuing to operate within an adversarial mindset despite the *McCrone Agreement* (SEED, 2001) and the EIS' positive partnership approach to CPD for teachers. This is best highlighted by both the local authorities and head teachers in many cases breaking the spirit and the letter of the law in terms of the statutory rights of LRs, particularly in relation to appropriate time-off for the representatives to effectively carry out their duties. Such actions are not sustainable in the long term and ignorance is not a defence as the statutory provisions and ACAS Code of Conduct (2003) have now been in force as of April 2003. The continuation of such behaviour may lead to legal repercussions that will result in legal precedents being set and acute embarrassment for the employers and head teachers alike.

The actions and attitudes of local authorities and head teachers affect the manner in which the LRs are able to operate effectively and they have been further hampered by CPD co-ordinators seeing them as a threat to their jobs. This is clearly not the case and was never the intention of the EIS to be so. This is another example of a breakdown in communication between the EIS and a key operational stakeholder and the situation must be addressed as a matter of urgency. The LRs are an additional resource for teachers to use and as Mathew MacIver (2006: 1-2) states the LRs have the credibility amongst their colleagues. At times teachers may in the first instance feel more comfortable seeking initial advice and guidance from the LRs rather than CPD co-ordinators or their head teachers, particularly if they have been out of the learning loop for any significant period of time.

However, there also seems to have been a breakdown in communication between the EIS and its members in terms of the LRs profile or in this case the distinct lack of one. This must be addressed as the lack of significant numbers of teachers coming through the door may affect the long-term sustainability of the LRs initiative. This may in part be down to the high proportion of new activists that are only now getting to grips with their role and responsibilities and in time will learn the "tricks of the trade" and raise their profile amongst colleagues. It may also have a lot to do with the cynicism with which teachers have greeted the new CPD developments, particularly CT. To a degree the latter is out of the control of the EIS and the LRs but both have a role to play in changing attitudes amongst the membership and show that current CPD initiatives are there to help teachers not hinder them.

Developing the Learning Representatives Initiative

The evidence presented in this book shows the EIS LRs are in part helping New Labour deliver the Learning Society, by brokering, facilitating and promoting the CPD of Scottish teachers. However, the EIS LRs policy trajectory is in danger of going off course significantly due to the non-connection with the operational stakeholders and the apathy and suspicion of Scottish teachers.

There are lessons from this case study that can be applied beyond the EIS and the Scottish education system. With this and the above overview in mind the stakeholders need to take decisive action if the LRs initiative is to progress and become an essential element of CPD within Scottish education. The following observations are designed to inform practice and should apply equally to other unions in the UK who can adapt them to their own circumstances.

In order for the LRs to gain the respect and recognition they deserve from within the EIS itself, particularly amongst local associations and members and secondly, from operational stakeholders, they must become part of the formal structures of the EIS and their position officially recognised in the Institute's constitution.

Post the completion of the University of Paisley's training module for LRs, the EIS must have a rolling programme of training that keeps the LRs up-to-date with developments and core skills, for example the media awareness course that was run recently. In addition, the University of Paisley should use the experiences of this cohort as examples of good and bad practice on its course. This will ensure that the LRs course is relevant and that students can not only relate theory to practice but will be fully aware of the practical obstacles that they will face once they have been accredited and are operational.

The key stakeholders in relation to the LRs, namely, the EIS, Scottish Executive, GTCS and LTS must run a road show for all operational stakeholders, namely, local authority education directors, head teachers and local authority and school CPD co-ordinators with three specific aims. Firstly, to clearly and definitively explain what the role and responsibilities of LRs are. Secondly to inform them of their legal obligations under the *Employment Act 2002* in relation to LRs both in terms of the spirit and letter of the law, particularly emphasising the importance of adequate time-off and facilities for LRs to effectively carry out their duties. Thirdly, that the LRs are not a threat (to the CPD co-ordinators) but another resource for both them and teachers to utilise as and when required. This must be presented in such a way as to not only highlight the partnership approach to learning as laid out by the Scottish Executive but also how it can benefit all the stakeholders at the operational level.

In addition to the above proposal the EIS within each local authority must run a series of meetings specifically targeted at teachers which will not only inform them about LRs but also sell the concept of CPD to them and clarify any misconceptions they have about professional development. As a matter of urgency all the key stakeholders should agree to publicise the positive aspects of CT and CPD for teachers, which in turn will hopefully encourage teachers to seek advice and guidance from the LRs.

All stakeholders need to show the teaching profession that they are serious about CPD for teachers and that it is not another initiative that will be lost in the mists of time. The stakeholders must address issues such as the provision of finance and adequate time for CPD; that CPD is not just about CT; CPD is about the personal as well as the professional development of teachers and that CPD for teachers is about working in partnership to ensure that both the individual teacher and their institution benefit from any professional development undertaken by teachers. The way forward may well be in the form of a Partnership Learning Agreement similar to the one agreed between Aberdeenshire Council and the EIS.

In turn the EIS and its LRs need to carefully consider the type of advice they give members. It is clear that this cannot be just CT driven and that if the LRs are to be effective in the long term they must stretch the boundaries of the advice and guidance they give. This can take the form of advising of courses that are more to do with personal development and well-being, which may in turn lead members to seek advice on more conventional CPD. This approach will also raise the profile of the LRs and has worked for other unions within teaching and other sectors.

Personal Reflections

From both a personal and professional perspective this study has broadened my horizons and thinking, particularly in terms of being an educational researcher. I have been through a period of self-reflection in relation as to how I conduct myself as a researcher based on my beliefs, ethics, values and research approach. I believe that this has had a positive effect and helped validate the whole process by ensuring the participants felt comfortable in sharing their views and opinions. Their voice has truly come to the fore in this book.

By adopting Ball's (1993) policy trajectory underpinned by Bowe et al's. (1992) context of policy making model it was possible to ensure the research sustained a direction and focus that interconnected policy issues in terms of formulation, interpretation, implementation and impact. I believe that if other academics and practitioners adopt this methodology it will help them make sense of policy in a more analytical and coherent manner.

The study has highlighted that there is a significant group

of people that are fully committed to the learning agenda, who are prepared to take on the responsibilities as LRs. Despite significant obstacles being put in their way they are helping colleagues to develop their professional skills and knowledge so they are now better able to positively impact on their pupils' development and learning.

I concur with Shelley (2005: 15) that curiosity pushes researchers to delve further and personally this is a key factor for me to continue to research and write on this subject to see how far and how big the EIS LRs and overall ULRs concept will become. So for me this is only the beginning of my journey in relation to researching and writing on the subject of EIS LRs and ULRs. The evidence suggests that the ULRs concept will continue to develop. It will have a significant impact on the learning agenda; continue to revitalise trade unions and create meaningful partnerships. Over time it may well heal the wounds of the industrial disputes of the 1970s and 1980s with the ultimate goal being better and more informed teacher practice that will impact positively on those that matter the most, the pupils.

References

Aberdeenshire Council and Educational Institute of Scotland (2005) *Partnership Learning Agreement*. Edinburgh: Educational Institute of Scotland.

Ackers, P. and Payne, J. (1998) British Trade Unions and Social Partnership: Rhetoric, Reality and Strategy in the *International Journal of Human Resource Management*, Volume 9, Number 3, pp. 529-550.

Advisory, Conciliation and Arbitration Service (2003) *Code of Practice on Time Off for Trade Union Duties and Activities*. London: Advisory, Conciliation and Arbitration Service.

Alexandrou, A. and Davies, J.D. (2005) Improving Police Probationer Training through a Democratic Research Process in Research in *Post-Compulsory Education*, Volume 10, Number 2, pp. 245-256.

Alexandrou, A., Davies, J.D. and Lee, J. (2005) Union Learning Representatives: A Case Study of the Public and Commercial Services Union in the *Journal of In-Service Education*, Volume 31, Number 1, pp. 9-26.

Alexiadou, N. and Ozga, J. (2002) Modernising Education Governance in England and Scotland: Devolution and Control in the *European Educational Research Journal*, Volume 1, Number 4, pp. 676-691.

Allan, J. (2003) Daring to think Otherwise? Educational Policymaking in the Scottish Parliament in the *Journal of Educational Policy*, Volume 18, Number 3, pp. 289-301.

Anderson, R. (2003) 'The History of Scottish Education, pre-1980', in Bryce, T.G.K. and Humes, W.M. (eds.) *Scottish Education, Second Edition, Post Devolution*, pp. 219-228. Edinburgh: Edinburgh University Press.

Ball, S.J. (1993) What Is Policy? Texts, Trajectories And Toolboxes in *Discourse*, Volume 13, Number 2, April, pp. 10-17.

Ball, S.J. (1994) What Is Criticism? A Continuing Conversation? A Rejoinder to Miriam Henry in *Discourse*, Volume 14, Number 2, April, pp. 108-110.

Bascia, N. (2000) The Other Side of the Equation: Professional Development and the Organizational Capacity of Teacher

Unions in *Educational Policy*, Volume 14, Number 3, July, pp. 385-404.

Belford, A. J. (1946) *Centenary Handbook Of The Educational Institute of Scotland.* Edinburgh: Educational Institute of Scotland.

Blair, T. (1996) *Age of Achievement for Britain.* A Speech by Tony Blair, Labour Party Leader at the Labour Party Conference. Blackpool, 1 October. London: Labour Party.

Bowe, R., Ball, S.J. and Gold, A. (1992) *Reforming Education and Changing Schools: Case Studies in Policy Sociology.* London: Routledge.

British Educational Research Association (2004) *Revised Ethical Guidelines for Educational Research.* Southwell: British Educational Research Association.

Brown, T. and England, J. (2005) Identity, Narrative and Practitioner Research: A Lacanian Perspective, in *Discourse*, Volume 26, Number 4, December, pp. 443-458.

Bryce, T.G.K. and Humes, W.M. (1999) *Policy Development in Scottish Education for the Scottish Parliament: Perspectives on Policy.* Glasgow: University of Strathclyde.

Calveley, M. (2005) *Teaching in Britain Today: Working in the Relegation Zone.* Glasgow: Humming Earth.

Calveley, M. and Healy, G. (2003) Political Activism and Workplace Industrial Relations in a UK 'Failing' School in the *British Journal of Industrial Relations*, Volume 41, Number 1, March, pp. 97-113.

Calveley, M., Healy, G., Shelley, S., Stirling, J. and Wray, D. (2003) *Union Learning Representatives – A Force for Renewal or 'Partnership'?* A paper presented at the 21st International Labour Process Conference, Bristol, 14-16 April.

Carter, B. (2004) State Restructuring and Union Renewal: The Case of the National Union of Teachers in *Work, Employment and Society*, Volume 18, Number 1, pp. 137-156.

Cassell, C. and Lee, B. (2005a) *The Trade Union View of the Union Learning Representative Initiative: A Research Report.* Sheffield: University of Sheffield Management School.

Cassell, C. and Lee, B. (2005b) *Comparing the Learning Representative Schemes of New Zealand and the UK: A Research Report.* Sheffield: University of Sheffield Management School.

Certification Officer (2007) *Annual Report of the Certification Officer: 2006-2007*. London: Certification Office for Trade Unions and Employers' Associations.
Chartered Institute of Personnel and Development (2004) *Trade Union Learning Representatives: The Change Agenda*. London: Chartered Institute of Personnel and Development.
Clough, B. (2005) *The Union Learning Representative – Challenges and Opportunities*. London: Trades Union Congress.
Clough, B. (2006) UnionLearn Research and Strategy Manager, *Interview*, March 8th.
Clough, B. (2007) *From Voluntarism to Post-Voluntarism: The Emerging Role of Unions in the Vocational Education and Training System*. London: UnionLearn.
Connelly, G. and McMahon (2007) Chartered Teacher: Accrediting Professionalism for Scotland's Teachers – A View from the Inside, in the *Journal of In-Service Education*, Volume 33, Number 1, pp. 91-105.
Cowen, G., Clements, M. and Cutter, J. (2000) *TUC Union Learning Representatives Survey*. Leeds: York Consulting.
Cutter, J., (2003) *Evaluation of SERTUC Activity*. Leeds: York Consulting.
Dehmel, A. (2005) *The Role of Vocational Education and Training in Promoting Lifelong Learning in Germany and England*. Didcot: Symposium Books.
Denzin, N.K. and Lincoln, Y.S. (2005) 'Paradigms and Perspectives in Contention', in Denzin, N.K. and Lincoln, Y.S. (eds.), *The Sage Handbook of Qualitative Research*, Third Edition, pp. 183-190. Thousand Oaks: Sage
Department for Education and Employment (1998) *The Learning Age – A Renaissance for a New Britain*. London: Department for Education and Employment.
Department for Education and Employment (1999) *Learning to Succeed – A New Framework for Post-16 Learning*. London: The Stationery Office.
Department for Education and Skills (2002) *Union Learning Fund – Year 6 Prospectus*. London: Department for Education and Skills.
Department for Trade and Industry and Department for Education

and Employment (2001) *Opportunity for All in a World of Change*. London: The Stationery Office.
Donnelly, E. and Kiely, J. (2007) *Union Learning Representatives: Championing Unions or (Just) Learning?* Bournemouth: Centre for Organisational Effectiveness, University of Bournemouth.
Draper, J., School of Education, University of Exeter, Senior Lecturer and Fast Track Co-ordinator (2006) *Interview*, 9th March
Draper, J. and Sharp, S. (2006) Continuity or Change? The Initial Impact of the Post-McCrone Agreement, *Scottish Educational Review*, Volume 37, Special Edition, January, pp. 100-113.
Educational Institute of Scotland (2003) *Scottish Union Learning Fund Bid Submission*. Edinburgh: Educational Institute of Scotland.
Educational Institute of Scotland (2005) *EIS Membership Figures, 2005*. Edinburgh: Educational Institute of Scotland.
Educational Institute of Scotland (2007) *EIS Membership Figures, 2007*. Edinburgh: Educational Institute of Scotland.
Edwards, A. (2002) Responsible Research: Ways of Being a Researcher in the *British Educational Research Journal*, Volume 28, Number 2, April, pp. 157-168.
Elliott, J., Kushner, S., Alexandrou, A., Davies, J.D., Wilkinson, S. and Zamorski, B. (2003) *Learning Requirement for Police Probationer Training in England and Wales*. Bristol and Norwich: UWE and UEA.
Enterprise and Lifelong Learning Committee (2002) *Final Report on Lifelong Learning*. 9th Report 2002, SP Paper 679. Edinburgh: Scottish Parliament.
Enterprise and Lifelong Learning Department (2001) *Inquiry by the Committee on Enterprise and Lifelong Learning*. Edinburgh: Scottish Parliament.
Etherington, K. (2004) *Becoming a Reflexive Researcher: Using Our Selves in Research*. London: Jessica Kingsley Publishers.
Fairley, J. (2003) 'The Enterprise and Lifelong Learning Department (ELLD) and the Scottish Parliament', in Bryce, T.G.K. and Humes, W.M. (eds.) *Scottish Education: Post Devolution*, Second Edition, pp. 132-140. Edinburgh: Edinburgh University Press.
Forrester, K. (2001) Modernised Learning: An Emerging Lifelong Agenda by British Trade Unions? in the *Journal of Workplace Learning*, Volume, 13, Number 7/8, pp. 318-325.

Forrester, K. (2004) 'The Quiet Revolution'? Trade Union Learning and Renewal Strategies in Work, *Employment and Society*, Volume, 18, Number 2, pp. 413-420.

Forrester, K. (2005) Learning for Revival; British Trade Unions and Workplace Learning in *Studies in Continuing Education*, Volume 27, Number 3, November, pp. 257-270.

Forrester, K. and Payne, J. (1999) 'A Sort of Metamorphosis': The Role of Trade Unions in Widening Participation in Lifelong Learning in *Widening Participation and Lifelong Learning*, Volume 1, Number 1, pp. 24-32.

Forrester, K. and Payne, J. (2000) Trade Union Modernisation and Lifelong Learning, in *Research in Post-Compulsory Education*, Volume 5, Number 2, pp. 153-171.

Friere, P. (1996) *Pedagogy of the Oppressed.* London: Penguin.

Fryer, R.H. (1997) *Learning for the 21st Century*. London: National Advisory Group for Continuing Education and Lifelong Learning.

Greckhamer, T. and Koro-Ljungberg, M. (2005) The Erosion of Method: Examples from Grounded Theory in the *International Journal of Qualitative Studies in Education*, Volume 18, Number 6, November-December, pp. 729-750.

Hammersley, M. (1994) 'Ethnography, Policy Making and Practice in Education' in Halpin, D. and Troyna, B. (Eds.) *Researching education Policy: Ethical and Methodological Issues*, pp 139-153. London: The Falmer Press.

Hammersley, M. (2005a) Countering the 'New Orthodoxy' in Educational Research: A Response to Phil Hodkinson in the *British Educational Research Journal*, Volume 31, Number 2, April, pp. 139-155.

Hammersley, M. (2005b) What can the Literature on Communities of Practice tell us about Educational Research? Reflections on some Recent Proposals in the *International Journal of Research & Method in Education*, Volume 28, Number 1, April, pp. 5-21.

Hammersley, M. and Atkinson, P. (1983) *Ethnography: Principles in Practice*. London: Tavistock Books.

Handy, C. (2001) *The Elephant and the Flea*. London: Hutchinson.

Haunch, P. and Bennett, T. (2002) *Organise, Educate and Agitate: Do Learning Partnerships help the Employer or Employee?* A Paper

Presented at the Canadian Industrial Relations Association's 39th Annual Conference – "Trade and Labour Protection: Can the Two be made to Work Together?", Toronto, 25-28 June.

Healy, G. (1999) The Trade Union Role in Career Development: A Membership Perspective in the *Industrial Relations Journal*, Volume 30, Number 3, pp. 212-228.

Heery, E., Healy, G. and Taylor, P. (2004) 'Representation at Work: Themes and Issues' in Healy, G., Heery, E., Taylor, P. and Brown, W. (eds.) *The Future of Worker Representation*, pp. 1-36. Basingstoke: Palgrave Macmillan.

Henry, M. (1993) What Is Policy? A Response to Stephen Ball in *Discourse*, Volume 14, Number 1, October, pp. 102-105.

Homan, R. (2002) 'The Principle of assumed Content: The Ethics of Gatekeeping' in McNamee, M. and Bridges, D., (eds.) *The Ethics of Educational Research*, pp. 23-40. Oxford: Blackwell Publishing.

Hoque, K. and Bacon, N. (2006) *Trade Union Recognition, Union Learning representatives and Training Incidence in Britain*. A paper presented at the 56th British Universities Industrial Relations Association Conference, Galway, 28-30 June.

House, E.R. (1980) *Evaluating with Validity*. Beverly Hills: Sage.

House, E.R. (1993) *Professional Evaluation: Social Impact and Political Consequences*. Newbury Park: Sage.

Howell, D.A. (1990) Some thoughts on researching 'grant-maintained schools' in the *Journal of Education Policy*, Volume 5, Number 3, pp. 242-244.

Humes, W.M. (2003) 'Policy Making in Scottish Education' in Bryce, T.G.K. and Humes, W.M. (eds.) *Scottish Education: Post Devolution*, Second Edition, pp. 74-85. Edinburgh: Edinburgh University Press.

Ironside, M. and Seifert, R. (1995) *Industrial Relations in Schools*. London: Routledge.

Johnson, A. (2007) A Speech by Alan Johnson Secretary of State for Education and Skills at the UnionLearn First Annual Conference, *One Year On*. London, 11 June. London: Department for Education and Skills. Available from http://www.dfes.gov.uk/speeches [Accessed 12 June 2007].

Johnston, D. and MacKenzie, M.L. (2003) 'The Politics of Scottish

Education' in Bryce, T.G.K. and Humes, W.M. (eds.) *Scottish Education: Post Devolution*, Second Edition, pp. 86-97. Edinburgh: Edinburgh University Press.

Kerchner, C.T. (2001) The Struggle for the Knowledge-Based Workplace in *The International Journal of Educational Management*, Volume 15, Number 5, pp. 220-237.

Kirk, G. (2000) *Enhancing Quality in Teacher Education*. Edinburgh: Dunedin Academic Press.

Kushner, S. (1992) *A Musical Education: Innovation in the Conservatoire*. Victoria: Deakin University Press.

Kushner, S. (2000) *Personalizing Evaluation*. London: Sage.

Labour Research Department (2001) *Learning at Work*. London: Labour Research Department.

Labour Research Department (2003) *Time Off for Trade Union Activities – A Guide for Workplace and Learning Reps*. London: Labour Research Department.

Labour Research Department (2005) *Teacher Union Learning Representatives – Promoting the Role of Teacher ULRs: A Guide for the Employers of Teachers*. London: Trade Union Fund South East.

Labour Research Department (2006) *Making a Real Difference – Union Learning Reps: A Survey*. London: UnionLearn.

Lee, B. and Cassell, C. (2004) Learning Representatives in UK Organizations: A Review of Current Developments in *Development and Learning in Organizations*, Volume 18, Number 4, pp 7-9.

Macaulay, S., Educational Institute of Scotland Assistant Secretary (2004) *Interview*, 6th October.

Macaulay, S. (2005) *Teaching Unions and the Learning Agenda: A Scottish Perspective*. A Paper presented at the International Professional Development Association Conference, *Continuing Professional Development: Who's Developing Whom?* Rednal, 9-10 December.

Macaulay, S. and Maclean, J. (2006) *Teaching Unions, the Learning Agenda and Partnership Working: The EIS Partnership with the University of Paisley*. A Paper Presented at the 5th Scottish Trade Union Network Research Conference. Glasgow, 2 June.

MacDonald, B. (1976) 'A Portrayal of Persons as Evaluation Data'.

A paper presented at the Annual Conference of the American Educational Research Association, San Francisco, as part of a symposium entitled *Issues and Methods in Qualitative Evaluation,* 23 April.

MacIver, M.M., General Teaching Council Scotland Chief Executive (2006) *Interview*, 24th February.

McClintock, L., Educational Institute of Scotland Learning Representatives Administrator (2004), *Interview*, 6th October.

McClintock, L. Educational Institute of Scotland Learning Representatives Administrator (2005) *Personal Record*, 16th August.

McCrone, G. (2000) *A Teaching Profession for the 21st Century*. Edinburgh: Scottish Executive.

McGiveny, V. (1999) *Excluded Men: Men who are Missing from Education and Training*. Leicester: National Institute of Adult Continuing Education.

McLeary, B., Learning and Teaching Scotland Chief Executive (2005) *Interview*, 22nd November.

McPherson, A. and Raab, C.A. (1988) *Governing Education – A Sociology of Policy Since 1945*. Edinburgh: Edinburgh University Press.

Menter, I., Mahony, P. and Hextall, I. (2004) Ne'er the Twain Shall Meet?: Modernizing the Teaching Profession in Scotland and England in the *Journal of Education Policy*, Volume 19, Number 2, March, pp. 195-214.

Miller, T. and Bell. (2002) 'Consenting to What? Issues of Access, Gate-Keeping and "Informed" Consent' in Mauthner, M. et al (eds.), *Ethics in Qualitative Research*, pp. 53-69. London: Sage Publications.

Moore, S. and Wood, H. (2007) *Union Learning, Union Recruitment and Organising*. London: UnionLearn.

Munro, A. and Rainbird, H. (2000) The New Unionism and the New Bargaining Agenda: UNISON-Employer Partnerships on Workplace Learning in Britain in the *British Journal of Industrial Relations*, Volume 38, Number 2, pp. 223-240.

Munro, A. and Rainbird, H. (2004a) Opening Doors as well as Banging on Tables: An Assessment of UNISON/Employer Partnerships on Learning in the UK Public Sector in the *Industrial Relations*

Journal, Volume 35, Number 5, pp. 419-433.
Munro, A. and Rainbird, H. (2004b) 'The Workplace Agenda – New Opportunities for Trade Unions in Healy, G., Heery, E., Taylor, P. and Brown, W. (eds.) *The Future of Worker Representation*, pp. 151-166. Basingstoke: Palgrave Macmillan.
National Literacy Trust (2003) *Union Learning Fund and the Role of Learning Representatives*. London: National Literacy Trust.
O'Brien, J., University of Edinburgh, School of Education Vice-Dean (2005) *Interview*, 22nd November.
Ozga, J. (1987) 'Part of the Union: School Representatives and their Work' in Lawn, M. and Grace, G. (eds.) *Teachers: The Culture and Politics of Work*, pp. 133-146. London: Falmer Press.
Parkinson, M. (1982) 'Politics and Policy-Making in Education' in Hartnett, A. (ed.) *The Social Sciences in Educational Studies*. London: Heinemann.
Parliament (2002) *Employment Act 2002*. London: The Stationery Office.
Paterson, L. (1998) The Civic Activism of Scottish Teachers: Explanations and Consequences, *Oxford Review of Education*, Volume 24, Number 3, pp 279-302.
Paterson, L. (2000) *Education and the Scottish Parliament*. Edinburgh: Dunedin Academic Press.
Paterson, L. (2005) *The Dilemmas of Education and of Democracy*. Edinburgh: Institute of Governance.
Payne, J. (1999) *Evaluation Report on the ISTC Union Learning Fund Project 1998/1999: Capacity Building in South Yorkshire*. Rotherham: Iron and Steels Trade Confederation.
Payne, J. (2000) *Final Evaluation Report – Graphical and Media Union Wessex Union Learning Fund Project 1999/2000: Sub-Regional Partnership in the Printing, Publishing and Packaging Industry: REACH – Regional Accord for Change:* Salisbury: Graphical Paper and Media Union.
Payne, J. (2001) What do Trade Unions Want from Lifelong Learning? In *Research in Post-Compulsory Education*, Volume 6, Number 3, pp. 355-373.
Phillips, D.C. (2004) 'Is "Mixed Methods Research" an Oxymoron?'. A paper presented at the Annual Conference of the American Educational Research Association, *Enhancing the Visibility and*

Credibility of Educational Research in San Diego, 12-16 April.

Poole, W.L. (2000) The Construction of Teachers' Paradoxical Interests by Teacher Union Leaders in the *American Educational Research Journal*, Volume 37, Number 1, Spring, pp. 93-119.

Purdon A. (2003) 'The Professional Development of Teachers', in Bryce, T.G.K. and Humes, W.M. (eds.) *Scottish Education, Second Edition, Post Devolution*, pp 942-951. Edinburgh: Edinburgh University Press.

Raab, C.D. (1994) 'Where Are We Now: Reflections on the Sociology of Education Policy' in Halpin, D. and Troyna, B. (eds.) *Researching Education Policy: Ethical and Methodological Issues*, pp. 17-30. London: The Falmer Press.

Rainbird, H. (2000) 'Training in the Workplace and Workplace Learning: Introduction' in Rainbird, H. (ed.) *Training in the Workplace*, pp. 1-17. Basingstoke: Macmillan Press.

Rainbird, H., Sutherland, J., Edwards, P., Holly, L. and Munro, A. (2003) *Employee Voice and Training at Work: Analysis of Case Studies and WERS 98*. Department for Trade and Industry, Employment Relations Research Series, Number 21. London: Department for Trade and Industry.

Rainbird, H., Munro, A. and Holly, L. (2004) 'The Employment Relationship and Workplace Learning' in Rainbird, H., Fuller, A. and Munro, A. (eds.) *Workplace Learning in Context*, pp. 38-53. London: Routledge.

Ross, C. (2000) *What Works? MSF, Lifelong Learning and the Workplace Representative*. Leeds: School of Continuing Education, University of Leeds.

Ross, C. (2001) *Promoting, Training and Supporting a Network of MSF Learning Representatives in Scotland.* Leeds: School of Continuing Education, University of Leeds.

Ruskin, J. (1869) *The Future of England.* A Lecture Delivered at the R.A. Institution, Woolwich, December 14.

Scott, J.K., Wishart, J.G. and Bowyer, D.J. (2006) Do Current Consent and Confidentiality Requirements Impede or Enhance Research with Children with Learning Disabilities? in *Disability & Society*, Volume 21, Number 3, May, pp. 273-287.

Scottish Executive (2003) *Life Through Learning Through Life.* Edinburgh: The Stationery Office.

Scottish Executive Education Department (2001) *A Teaching Profession for the 21st Century: Agreement Reached Following the McCrone Report*. Edinburgh: The Stationery Office.
Scottish Office (1998) *Opportunity Scotland: A Paper on Lifelong Learning*. Cm 4048. Edinburgh: The Stationery Office.
Scottish Office (1999) *Developing Skills for Employability*. Edinburgh: The Stationery Office.
Scottish Parliament (2000) *Standards in School Act 2000*. Edinburgh: The Stationery Office.
Scottish Trades Union Congress (2005) *Unions Work for Learning – A Profile of Trade Union Learning in Scotland*. Glasgow: Scottish Trades Union Congress.
Seddon, T. (1996) The principle of choice in policy research in the *Journal of Education Policy*, Volume 11, Number 2, pp197-214.
Shelley, S. (2005) *Working in Universities: From Porter to Professor*. Glasgow: Humming Earth.
Shelley, S. (2006) *Multiple Partnerships in Trade Union Learning*. A paper presented at the 56th British Universities Industrial Relations Association Conference, Galway, 28-30 June.
Smith, K. (2003) *The Learning Rep – A New Trade Union Role*. A paper presented at the 53rd British Universities Industrial Relations Association Conference. Leeds, 3-5 July.
Soobrayan, V. (2003) Ethics, Truth and Politics in Constructivist Qualitative Research in *Westminster Studies in Education*, Volume 26, Number 2, October, pp. 107-123.
Stake, R.E. (2004) *Standards-Based & Responsive Evaluation*. Thousand Oaks: Sage.
Stake, R.E. (2005) 'Qualitative Case Studies' in Denzin, N.K. and Lincoln, Y.S. (eds.) *The Sage Handbook of Qualitative Research*, Third Edition, pp. 443-466. Thousand Oaks: Sage.
Stevenson, H. (2003) On the Shopfloor: Exploring the Impact of Teacher Trade Unions on School-Based Industrial Relations in *School Leadership & Management*, Volume 23, Number 3, August, pp. 341-356.
Stevenson, H. (2005) From 'School Correspondent' to Workplace Bargainer? The Changing Role of the School Union Representative in the *British Journal of Sociology of Education*, Volume 26,

Number 2, April, pp. 219-233.

Stevenson, H. (2007) Restructuring Teachers' Work and Trade Union Responses in England: Bargaining for Change? in the *American Educational Research Journal*, Volume 44, Number 2, June, pp. 224-251.

Stuart, M. (2004) *Trade Union Learning Representatives in Britain: Policy Innovation in VET*. A paper presented at the Centre for the Economics of Education and Training, Monash University's 8th National Conference, *The Policy Context for Education and Training*. Melbourne, 29 October.

Stuart, M. and Robinson, A. (2007) *Training, Union Recognition and Collective Bargaining: Findings from the 2004 Workplace Employment Relations Survey*. London: UnionLearn.

Stuart, M., Wallis, E. and Greenwood (2003) *Trade Union Learning Representatives in South Yorkshire*. Leeds: Leeds University Business School, University of Leeds.

Sutherland, J. and Rainbird, H. (2000) 'Unions and Workplace Learning: Conflict or Cooperation with the Employer' in Rainbird, H. (ed.) *Training in the Workplace*, pp. 189-209. Basingstoke: Macmillan Press.

Terry, M. (2003) Can 'Partnership' Reverse the Decline of British Trade Unions? in *Employment and Society*, Volume 17, Number 3, pp. 459-472.

Thompson, P., Warhurst, C. and Findlay, P. (2007) *Organising to Learn and Learning to Organise: Three Case Studies on the Effects of Union-Led Workplace Learning*. London: UnionLearn.

Thursfield, D., Holden, R. and Hamblett, J. (2004) Learning Brokers in the Workplace: A Typology of Practice in *Research in Post-Compulsory Education*, Volume 9, Number 3, pp. 371-388.

Trades Union Congress (2001) *The Smart Set – Union Learning Reps at Work*. London: Trades Union Congress.

Trades Union Congress (2003) *ULRs Perceptions of New Learning Through Work*. London: Trades Union Congress.

Trades Union Congress Learning Services Task Group (1998) *Learning Services Task Group Report*. London: Trades Union Congress.

Troyna, B. (1994) 'Reforms, Research and Being Reflexive About Being Reflective', in Halpin, D. and Troyna, B. (eds.) *Researching Education Policy: Ethical and Methodological Issues*, pp. 1-14.

London: The Falmer Press.
Vincenzi, C. and Fairhurst, J. (2002) Law *and the European Community*, Third Edition. London: Longman.
Waddington, J. (1995) UK Unions: Searching for an Agenda in *Transfer*, Volume 1, Number 1, pp.31-43.
Walford, G. (2005) Research Ethical Guidelines and Anonymity in the *International Journal of Research & Method in Education*, Volume 28, Number 1, April, pp. 83-93.
Wallis, E. and Stuart, M. (2007) *A Collective Learning Culture: A Qualitative Study of Workplace Learning Agreements*. London: UnionLearn.
Wallis, E., Stuart, M. and Greenwood, I. (2005) 'Learners of the Workplace Unite!': An Empirical Examination of the UK Trade Union Learning Representative Initiative, *Work, Employment and Society*, Volume 19, Number 2, pp 283-304.
Weiss, C.H. (1998) *Evaluation*, Second Edition. Upper Saddle River: Prentice Hall.
Wilson, A. (2005) 'Message from Allan Wilson' in *Unions Work for Learning – A Profile of Trade Union Learning in Scotland.* Glasgow: STUC.
Wood, H. and Moore, S. (2005) *An Evaluation of the UK Union Learning Fund – Its Impact on Unions and Employers*. London: Working Lives Research Institute, London Metropolitan University.

Index

Printed in the United Kingdom
by Lightning Source UK Ltd.
128245UK00001B/355-402/A

9 781846 220135